Luke, Stranger
Outsiders in Luke's Gospel

Rob Atkins

2020

For the Powers family, past, present and future

Rob Atkins is a freelance French and piano teacher. He is the author of 'Abertillery Kid' and 'Playing at the Roxy' and a singer songwriter with the folk band Frost at Midnight.

Jesus the Great Includer and the Great Outsider

'Luke, Stranger' is not really a Bible commentary. It's more a longish meditation on a theme as it appears in one Bible book. I thought I'd look at Luke's gospel, concentrating on the way Jesus is interested in including and identifying with all kinds people who were often excluded in his day.

My interest came about in this way: I'd often looked at outsiders in Luke's gospel before, noticing Jesus bringing back people into the Judaism of his day - people like publicans and prostitutes - but one year just before the summer holidays I decided to cast the net a bit wider and underline the compassion of Jesus towards all the outsiders I could identify in the book. I thought I'd jump into the middle of the gospel and pick stories at random and there might be four or five. I was thinking at that early stage about Samaritans and prodigals but, I suppose out of a sense of duty, I started looking at the beginning of the gospel. A couple of years later, I was still going strong but by that time I was 'outside the camp' myself - not a serving Baptist minister any longer but still concerned with the outsider, the stranger. I found out that there is plenty going on outside the four walls of church buildings as far as God is concerned.

I was a Baptist minister in France for well over ten years and when I came back home to the United Kingdom in 2002, some new opportunities presented themselves. One of those was to lead a seminar in Church History at Cardiff University. There's a Latin proverb that says 'you learn by teaching' and I can testify to that. One of the things I learned is that the story of the Church is all too often one of power and domination. Across the centuries, macho leaders have been ready to exclude and silence others and to fight, often physically, for their beliefs to prevail. For every St Francis with his embrace of vulnerability and poverty, there seem to be a dozen inquisitors and monarchs turning the story of Christianity into a political tale. I've learned that Church history is often a story about influential braggarts with loud voices who make sure there is no advocate for the quieter soul. It's a story about men. For every woman whose name we remember with gratitude there are a dozen lesser men demanding our attention.

Where did Christians learn this behaviour and these emphases? Where did all this power-hungry empire building come from? Well, unfortunately the Bible as a whole contains many an example of patriarchy, corruption and violence, all done in God's name. It's an interesting exercise to read the Bible through with the word 'power' in mind. From such a reading, it's clear that personally ambitious, empire-building Christians have plenty to build on but one place you won't find much in this vein is Luke's gospel. It is the gospel for the underdog, the outsider, the powerless, the alien, the stranger. So, I've decided to call this book, 'Luke, Stranger'. That's a nod to W.H. Auden's poem, 'Look, Stranger' but the title also contains a friendly and welcoming address to the stranger and even a suggestion that Luke himself as a Gentile among Jews may be one of those very outsiders he wants to encourage with the message of Jesus - the Great Includer.

The Bible is a Book About Strangers
From start to finish, the Bible is a book about strangers and refugees. In the beginning, Adam and Eve are obliged to leave the Garden of Eden and prevented from returning by a flashing, flaming sword. Their exile is not only from a place but also from a state - one of blissful innocence and immediate communion with God. From now on, their lot is more difficult and it quickly involves their children in quarrelling and in death and wandering. The Tower of Babel is a search for permanence that ends not only in confusion of language but in scattering.

Aged Abraham leaves his home in exchange for decades of seeking for a land of promise - he experiences the grief of childlessness as a well as the joys and frustrations of fatherhood. Egypt -the biblical place of refuge, temptation and separation - makes its first appearance of many in the story of Sarah and Abraham.

The descendants of Abraham and Sarah are no strangers to

sojourning and to biding their time: Rebecca and Rachel, Isaac and Jacob know all about this lifestyle while Joseph has slavery and imprisonment to contend with as well, until he is set free to save his family from famine. Their salvation involves a journey to settle in Egypt once again.

The King who knew not Joseph made the Israelites remember their status as strangers and, again over a period of decades rather than months of suffering, God made ready two brothers, Moses and Aaron to bring his deliverance. Even then, a period of wandering in the desert was the lot of practically all those who left Egypt with so much hope. They nearly all died without seeing the Promised Land, including Moses himself. It was Joshua who took the people over the Jordan.

Surely this is an end to the story of wandering and of the tale of God's people as refugees? Certainly, a capital city was established along with a centre of worship. Even that act of settlement was done by a king called David who had known what it was to hide in caves and even serve the army of the national enemy while he was being pursued by Saul. He was a stranger and a refugee, too.

The hold of the Israelites over the land was precarious and first the Assyrian 'came down like a wolf on the fold' and swept away the people of the northern part of the kingdom, never to be seen again. Next, Babylon took the cream of Jerusalem to serve in a foreign land -

people of the intellectual and spiritual stature of Daniel and Ezekiel. It was a short exile in biblical terms before Cyrus the Persian resettled Jerusalem but it was an exile nonetheless. With the rebuilding of the Holy City the Old Testament ends.

Leaving aside John the Baptist who lived off any reasonable scale of poverty, it is a commonplace to say that Jesus himself was a refugee. At Christmas, we hear about Mary and Joseph forced to leave their home for Mary to give birth to the Saviour in poor circumstances. It has been said that, 'Jesus was born in an oil drum in the garage because there was no room in the pub.' The first visitors to Jesus in the manger were the shepherds who took care of the flocks of another in all weathers. T.S. Eliot wrote about the 'cold coming' of the Magi to Bethlehem but really those words are more applicable to the shepherds. Even after this squalid beginning, the ordeal of the Holy Family was not at an end as yet more time in Egypt beckoned. This time, Mary and Joseph and the baby were on the run from Herod, a tyrant king on the rampage.

Jesus told of his own experience as an adult like this: 'Foxes have holes and the birds of the air have nests but the Son of Man has nowhere to lay his head.' That's his outward existence but theologically, there is a great richness in the thought that the earthly life of Jesus was one of exile from God's presence. I have reflected often that his emptying of himself to serve us involved Jesus in a limitation of himself. There is much to be gained from a meditation on how he set about maintaining his communion with God while far from home. Even his final words on the Cross speak to this sense of distance: 'My God, my God, why have you forsaken me?' The apostles thought deeply about this mystery and Paul said, 'Though he was rich, for your sakes he became poor, so that in him you may become the riches of God'.

The first followers of Jesus would have loved to settle down, it seems. Jesus told them to go to the whole world with the message of the Kingdom of God but they stayed in Jerusalem and it took a great persecution to scatter them. In an astonishing twist, one of the persecutors became a restless traveller for the gospel when he was converted to Christ. Paul was a tent maker who probably made good use of his own product. He certainly experienced the misery of shipwreck and being cast away on strange shores as he wandered all over the known world with always the desire to go where the message had never before been preached and in spite of the blows and beatings and contradiction that awaited him wherever he went.

The New Testament ends with a man called John in exile as a stranger on the island of Patmos where he sees that there can be no continuing city for any Christian before the new Jerusalem comes down from heaven, all things are made new and there are no more strangers and no more wandering.

What to say to Refugees

I made six journeys to see some friends in France who were working with the refugees in the Calais Jungle. I've dedicated this book to the Powers family, past and present and I hope many of the children will read this, think about Uncle Josh and smile someday. Chuck and Cathy Powers are Americans who were involved in work with the homeless in Toulouse at the same time as I was and our friendship goes back well over twenty years. It is their concern for the homeless which took them from the sunny south of France to the north near Boulogne. They had welcomed a homeless man called René Vasseur into their household in Toulouse and when he died they felt called to move elsewhere to work with his family in a run-down township in the north of France called Desvres. Desvres was once famous as the fancy porcelain capital of France but no one buys that kind of thing now except when the piece is antique.

The Powers family is not inclined to ignore human need right on the doorstep and when the refugee crisis and the Calais Jungle began to make headline news they had already been involved for a long time, going into the camp on at least a weekly basis and bringing men to church on a Sunday morning in their own beat-up car. There was worship followed by a shared meal and then the men went back to their nightmare conditions.

When they moved up to Boulogne, I thought it would be a

good idea to visit the Powers family occasionally and I have been a good few times over the years. What deters me from going more often is not the channel crossing or driving on the right but the interminable journey from South Wales to Dover via the London orbital motorway. The refugee crisis gave me a real reason to go regularly and each time I took a car full of clothes and non-perishable food items people in my part of Wales were kind enough to donate.

Each time I went there was an opportunity to speak with refugees, from Sudan, Ethiopia or Iran. Some of them are Christians and it would be a mistake to see them as babes in Christ longing for basic teaching. In fact, when I went in October 2016, there was a large Christian meeting in the camp from which many of the listeners returned disappointed because of the elementary level of what had been shared. The people I have met love to sing Christian songs even though the guitars they have are usually missing a few strings. These strangers are friendly and hospitable and always willing to share what food they have with visitors. Once, I took in a big bag of onions and was rewarded with a succulent lamb dinner in return.

Sometimes, I was able to speak informally in the tents and makeshift shelters. Once, in that setting, I was invited to share about my own Christian journey and I found myself reflecting on the way God leads us in the long term rather than on any spectacular signs or specific guidance I may have experienced. I told them of how my studies in French at university and my piano lessons as a boy with the elderly lady up the road as well as a doctorate in theology and thirty years of church ministry had brought me to that particular group of Iranian refugees in all of their insecurity. I found myself encouraging them with the thought that, under God, life is long and that the Calais Jungle is just one place and one time among many in their earthly pilgrimage. Other times and other places will become possible for them, whether back in Teheran, in London or New York or who knows where.

On each occasion that I've been to France I've had a chance to preach in French in the Baptist Church in Boulogne. I usually take an aspect of my favourite theme of the stranger in Luke's gospel but once I decided to address the refugees in the congregation directly. I chose to speak about the passage in Jeremiah where the prophet writes a letter to the exiles in Babylon. Jeremiah's message is applicable to refugees today. When I talk about the Calais Jungle here in Wales, I often get a sense that there is fear just below the surface in the person or the group I am talking to. That fear is often pinned to a vague idea that some of the people I am helping may turn out to be terrorists. It so happens that I have seen nothing personally to feed into that fear, but in any case, Jeremiah tells refugees how they are to behave. He tells the exiles in Babylon not to work for the overthrow of the country where they are settled but instead to work for its prosperity, because if the host country prospers, the guests prosper as well.

It so happens that I am one of those who tend to see immigration not as a threat to social cohesion but as a promise of richness and depth for our communities. In fact, I miss the days when I served congregations in France made up of many nationalities and bearing witness to what the apostle Peter in one of his letters calls the 'multi-coloured' grace of God.

The Meaning of life

On 11th November 1979 I stood with Patrick, my landlord, on the balcony of his flat in *rue du 11 novembre* in Caen, Normandy. A great procession with bands and ranks of soldiers and veterans was taking place in the square where the war memorial stands, overlooked by a hotel which had been the Nazi headquarters during the Occupation of France. Patrick said to me casually as we watched, 'They are remembering the only time they were really alive.'

That chance remark has stayed with me ever since. Often, I have wondered what the most important cause of our time is - the one which would give meaning to a life today in the way that the struggle against Hitler did for that earlier generation. I have found great fulfilment in working with homeless people and in putting on concerts to raise money for those involved in terrible natural disasters. All the same, that great over-arching sense of purpose has eluded me. May

God forbid that fascism rises again in my lifetime to provide a suitable target for my efforts.

In the Bible, Esther - yet another member of God's people in exile - has won a beauty contest. The king's wife had defied her lord and, according to the laws of the time, she had to be replaced by a more compliant spouse. Esther had won that honour. The story is quickly told. A plot to kill the Israelites has been uncovered and Mordecai, Esther's kinsman, points out to her that only she has access to the king to plead her people's cause. He tells her, 'If you keep silent, then relief for the people will come from another quarter but who knows if you have come to royal power for such a time as this?'

'Such a time as this'. Today, millions of people are on the move because of trouble in their own countries. The refugees I met in the Calais Jungle may have fled from genocide in Darfur or they may have been persecuted for Christian faith in Iran or in Syria but it all adds up to the greatest humanitarian crisis since the Second World War. It seems to me that from a purely human point of view, we must help to alleviate the suffering of those caught up in these terrible events and that our efforts, no matter what they might be, may well give our lives a sense of meaning and purpose.

As Christians, though, we should realise that God's call to us at such a time as this has yet greater urgency and is a matter of faith. First, many of these displaced people are our brothers and sisters in

Christ and we are to treat them as we would treat Christ himself and help them in any way we can. That appeal is clearly set out in what Jesus says about the sheep and the goats in Matthew 24. Of course, not all the refugees are Christians but Chuck Powers, my American friend in Desvres has a second argument which he expresses forcefully and which I find very convincing: 'Man', he says with great excitement, 'the mission agencies spend millions of dollars sending missionaries to these countries and here they are on our doorstep for the price of a tank of gas!'

Just one man

I always look forward to watching the war film 'The Great Escape' over the holiday season. There's an unspectacular scene in that movie where one of the British prisoners of war is lecturing to some of the others on how to recognise different kinds of birdsong. Amongst other things and in spite of the hardship, the POW camps provided many educational opportunities because of the varied expertise of the detainees with time on their hands and knowledge to impart.

I think the Calais Jungle was like that. In fact, a young man called Banya told me so when I met him over coffee in the Powers home. In the camp, you could learn anything you had a mind to. In his case, he studied languages and now speaks five others including his native Kurdish. Farsi, Arabic and English he learned from his fellows in the camp. Many of us too easily take it for granted that everyone in the world must be able to speak English and we should realise that the ability to speak a number of languages is the norm from which we native anglophones tend to deviate.

Banya is a resourceful and engaging young man with a good sense of humour. Understandably, he is a little wary in conversation at first but he soon opens up about his experience. The difficulties faced by Kurdish people in northern Iraq and in Syria are well-known but the Calais Jungle turned out to be a refuge in spite of its hardships. When the camp was destroyed, Banya was able to escape with a caravan. It was only going to be towed away to be burned by the authorities anyway.

Now, the Powers family has allowed Banya to put the caravan in their garden and it is a colourful addition to the bustling household. On the Saturday evening when I was there, I put on a concert as my French-speaking alter-ego Bobby Tivoli and Banya and Michelle provided the food. As far as I am concerned, a kebab is just some meat on a skewer but that's not what these resourceful chefs had in mind. I tasted the chicken concoction in the pan and couldn't believe how tangy it was. It's all in the lemons, apparently and many times since I've tried to reproduce the dish, sometimes with some success.

Banya is now part of the church in Desvres, too - he has been baptised and although he has no idea of what the future will hold, he openly says that he wants to serve God. I think he'll make a great contribution to the world wherever he manages to settle. There are thousands of strangers like him on the move and I feel that on the whole they are an asset, not a threat.

Game of Thrones   (Luke 1 and 2)
When Princess Elizabeth became Queen in 1952 and particularly around the time of the Coronation in Westminster Abbey a year later there was a renewal of interest in the first Elizabethan age of the sixteenth century. It was a selective reading of that time, of course: people were not really interested in the squalor or the political uncertainty of those times but revelled in the largely fictional majesty and confidence of the earlier epoch.

In the first couple of chapters of Luke's gospel, we are in an olde-worlde setting and we are treated to a selective re-reading of the Old Testament as the main themes of the whole book are set out in one place. Once a year, when the regular accompanist goes on holiday I get a chance to play the piano for a choir in a village called St Briavels on the fringe of the wild and mysterious Forest of Dean. This year, they were doing 'HMS Pinafore' and I was a bit nervous as I sat down to practise because it's not a Gilbert and Sullivan opera I know well. That feeling of trepidation turned to relief as I played through the first act because I found I knew much of the music already from a record of the overture I enjoyed as a teenager. Many of the main tunes are set out in one go: granted, there will be some new melodies but at least the audience can hum along to something they recognise from what the orchestra was playing as they settled into their seats. The first two chapters of Luke are like an overture - as the book unfolds there will be new material aplenty but there will also be much that will be familiar from the first two chapters.

At the start of Luke there are four big speeches given by Zechariah, Mary, the Christmas angels and the aged Simeon in the Jerusalem Temple. They are often called by their Latin names - Benedictus, Magnificat, Gloria and Nunc Dimittis - and the theme of each of them is promise and fulfilment. God made promises in the Old Testament which are fulfilled in Christ and by the creative power of the Holy Spirit, emphasised in every part of this introductory material.

So, just as the Spirit of God brooded over the waters in Genesis, God's creative power makes life from old people like Elizabeth and Zechariah, the parents of John the Baptist and even from nothing in the case of Mary, the mother of Jesus. Similarly, God intervenes in the sacrificial system gone stale and brings a new word to the aged priest, Zechariah. There is even an echo of the garden of Eden as Zechariah questions God's message just as Adam and Eve did. It takes a Mary to open the way to the future by an open acceptance of that new word from God and availability to it.

The fact that it is Mary who is the first to react in that way is significant, as is the content of what she says. If we thought Christianity was all about men, exploitation, money, luxury and power, here is a rebuttal in the first few pages of Luke. Women are among the first to speak in Luke and Mary seems to be channelling some of the few female voices in the Old Testament rising from the clamour of patriarchy to sing of God's justice for the downtrodden. Mary is Ruth and Hannah; she is Deborah and Myriam and she sings the song of reversals and the world turned upside down. Her theme is God's concern for the humble and his preference for working with ordinary people rather than those at the top, however that is interpreted in our context.

In his overture, Luke sets out his themes. As we go through the gospel we will meet the waiting faithful, the powerless and excluded and those of little worth in the eyes of the world. They will meet Jesus - or in some cases Jesus will tell their tale in a vivid word picture - and they will find their voice and their place of honour in Church history. If the theme of this overture is promise and fulfilment, the gospel as a whole will show the outworking of that.

In one church where I served for well over ten years there were three ornate carved chairs which were set out for the minister and two members of the leadership team at the monthly service of the Lord's Supper. The two on either side were already quite impressive and meant to convey status in the Fellowship but they were as nothing compared with the minister's throne with its cushions and intricate woodwork on the back and armrests. Sometimes, when I remembered to do it, I would replace this seat just before the service with an ordinary plastic stacking chair from the back room. I was making a point about ministry as service, of course, but as I went on looking at Luke's gospel I began to think of this action as a picture of the gospel as a whole.

Biographical Pain   (Luke 2:22-30)
I once attended a conference on old age and I met two aged people called Simeon and Anna there. Because of my immersion in Luke's gospel I was already thinking about the excluded and those without power and the discussion that day helped me realise that there is probably no group in our society that fits this description better than the elderly. I am fortunate enough to live in a close and supportive village community in South Wales but all the same many of its residents are never to be seen outside or in fact by anyone much, apart from the faithful carers doing their rounds.

Of course, old age can be a time of fulfilment and the bearing of fruit and the Bible often talks about that aspect of ageing: for one psalmist, white hair is a crown of glory and another likens the elderly believer to a tree bearing fruit to the end. When old age goes in another direction, though, it can make us very fearful for ourselves as we grow old. As for those we love, some of the things we see can leave us upset and troubled or the person concerned. I'm sorry to have to say that this is how it was with both my parents not too long ago. As one contributor to the conference on ageing put it, a pleasant muddle becomes a return to chaos and confusion; a mild irritation becomes a fear-fuelled aggression; a sense of completion and a final affirmation of the identity becomes a loss of self; a sense of community and connection becomes a sense of isolation and, yes, of exclusion as the well-known person becomes a stranger. I have wondered on many occasions when I have sat with those at the end of life where the person I knew has gone and in what sense the person will be restored when God makes all things new.

It so happens that shortly after this conference I was so eager to talk about Simeon and Anna that I did it on Pentecost Sunday. This might seem an eccentric choice given that Pentecost is usually held to be about the apostles and the birthday of the Church. Well, I've already written about how the opening of Luke's gospel is rooted in the Old Testament and the action of the Holy Spirit in those times. Just as the Holy Spirit moved on the waters to bring the world and its wonders into existence, the Holy Spirit moves to bring new life into people like the elderly Elizabeth and the Virgin Mary. And the Holy Spirit is active in the lives of the aged Simeon and Anna - Luke is at great pains to make that clear. Books were not usually illustrated in Luke's day and short of using italics, underlining and capital letters, he couldn't do more than he does to draw attention to the part played by the Holy Spirit.

So, for Luke, Simeon and Anna have their longing, the ancient disciplines of Judaism and the Holy Spirit. I went to a seminar at the conference and in a sobering moment we were in a circle and we had to say how we would like to die. People were talking about beautiful music and poetry and the company of friends and family, so I began putting together a similar answer until a professor of gerontology began to speak about what he called 'biographical pain'. He said that what you really want as you come to the end of life is resolution and a sense of fulfilment and I found myself agreeing more with him than I did with the others with their Mozart and Wordsworth.

This fulfilment is exactly what the Holy Spirit gives Simeon and Anna in the Temple. As we listen to them speaking, we see that any chaos or confusion, any irritation or hurt at having lived so long and seen so little, is healed and resolved by the coming of the Messiah. Simeon and Anna, people who have lost connection with their society become representatives of those who have lived so long and endured so much that they have lived to see the personification of God's promises to Israel in Jesus Christ. The Holy Spirit gave them that fulfilment.

At Pentecost, we often focus so much on the spectacular coming of the Spirit and the astonishing expansion of the Church that we forget two things that are perhaps more relevant to our own lives: that the Spirit is the author of every good thing in our Christian lives - fruits and gifts, faith, hope and love - and that the Spirit is still wanting to bring people to a sense of fulfilment, completion and resolution at the end of life today.

So, what about the exclusion, the loss of power, the frailty, the poverty of old age? Well, I'm glad I went to the conference because I heard many thought-provoking things, not least this: In the gospels, Jesus put the child in the midst of his followers and told them that if they want to enter the kingdom, they should be like little children. It was suggested that if Jesus were here to minister today (and he is, naturally) he might place an elderly person there in the circle instead of a child.

This is quite controversial and I've been mulling it over for some time. I'll go just a little bit further. I'm not a Roman Catholic but on the back of my doctorate on French Catholicism I am a bit of a Vatican-watcher and as I observed the final years of Pope John-Paul II and listened to people talking about his apparent loss of dignity and clamouring for his discreet resignation, I didn't agree but I couldn't quite say why. My conference helped me understand that an elderly person in all his or her powerlessness and frailty can be a strong image of dependence on God. This, too, may be part of God's way with any of us and it seems to me that the Pope was showing that even this aspect of so many lives can be included in God's providence in our pilgrimage.

For this to be true, we need the Holy Spirit to be active in our existence. Clearly, he is active in the strength and vibrancy of the young nurse, the enthusiastic teacher or the dynamic missionary striding the globe with the gospel but he is also in the dark Temple at the end of two long lives, those of Simeon and Anna, as the Holy Spirit brings fulfilment in Christ. The Holy Spirit is active in the houses of the forgotten in our community, in the home for the elderly and in the hospital room as a life ebbs away.

Utopia (Luke 3:1-22)
I'm looking forward to writing about the Nazareth Manifesto - the time when Jesus in his home synagogue declared himself to be on the side of the weak - but first we need to look at John the Baptist's teaching to the crowds coming to be baptised by him. What with the promise of his birth, his unusual lifestyle and the injustice of his death, we're familiar with John's life story but the challenge of his preaching and the way it addresses the predicament of the oppressed is less well-known. Perhaps we hurry past it with a little too much eagerness to reach the ministry of Jesus. We know from the Bible and

secular history that many very honourable seekers after God were happy to be identified as followers of John well into the time of the Church.

Luke is a great teacher and he distils what must have been many hours of teaching by John into just three situations that arose when specific groups in society came to ask him questions about how to conduct their lives. This is important: God is interested in us and how we live to the extent that he prefers us to act in particular ways. John was clear about that and was quite happy to inform people about God's perspective. His prescriptions are down-to-earth, maybe uncomfortably so. He doesn't talk about going to church, praying more or reading the Bible but about the details of daily living.

'What shall we do?' is the crowd's enquiry and John answers directly by telling people to have a lifestyle based on consideration for those in need. Of course, somebody is going to jump in and say that this is a gospel of good works and that a gospel based on human endeavour never saved anyone. That's true, and in fact it's one of my instincts to have that thought, but I need to remember that there is a gracious lifestyle that comes out of right believing and that the Bible shows that the Christian message involves a lifestyle that can be observed as well as a set of teachings that can be heard and studied.

I'm a great fan of charity shops and once I ended up with two beautiful winter coats for practically no money. I couldn't wear them both so I gave one away. It would be foolish of me to think that I'd fulfilled the spirit of the first part of John's teaching by obeying his word to the letter. The correct interpretation is that if I'm living in relative wealth and I can see that there's need anywhere in the world that I can satisfy or work with others to alleviate, I need to be prepared to share. I shouldn't be doubling up on possessions if there are those who have none. I suppose that puts paid to my ever having a second home in the South of France.

Next on the scene are tax collectors. It's interesting that John the Baptist doesn't condemn them outright and say that money has no place in God's economy. Later on we'll see that money is the second biggest theme in the teaching of Jesus after the Kingdom of God and that even Jesus himself doesn't try to evade the taxes that belong to the Temple - although it doesn't fall to many of us to pay our taxes with money found in the mouth of a fish!

I was in the bank recently moving money from one heaving account to another and the man behind the counter said, 'There's no reason for anyone to pay tax anymore.' He meant that if you are astute, you can keep that money moving around in mid-air so that the Chancellor of the Exchequer can't get his hands on it. I'm sure that's true but if I'd had my wits about me, I'd have shared my convictions with him and told him, 'I love to pay tax, I want better healthcare, free education for all and compassionate and generous social security for those less fortunate than I am.' I missed that opportunity, although that's exactly what I did say to my daughter who is new to the world of work when she asked why she has to pay taxes when others evade theirs. John is succinct. We know from elsewhere in the gospel that in New Testament times, to be a tax collector was usually to live on extortion and backhanders. John says that tax collectors shouldn't take more than their due and that's it.

The third and last group of people on the scene are soldiers. This is a bit of a shock because in an ideal world there is no need for the military at all but if you are expecting John to launch a tirade against the oppressive Roman forces, you'll be disappointed. He doesn't tell them to desert or to turn their arms on their own rulers. He simply tells them not to take part in looting and not to exploit those they are asked to police. The issue of just or unjust war John does not address at all.

There's something missing, of course and John himself concludes what he has to say by pointing forward to Jesus who will bring whole other dimensions in a spiritual sense not only by putting us right with God but also by purifying the world in a radical way. In many ways we still wait for this and in the meantime, there is still poverty, still economics and still fighting. The title of one of Francis Shaeffer's influential books is 'How should we then live?' The teaching of John the Baptist shows that in a world of very visible need this is not a theoretical question but one with a visible outworking. The question addressed by Francis Shaeffer and by John the Baptist won't go away any time soon so we had better have a go at answering them while there is still time for us.

Putting Bread on the Table (Luke 3:23-28)
Serving as a kind of bridge between the olde-worlde first two chapters of Luke and the gospel proper is the genealogy and if there are any parts of the Bible we tend to skip over, they are the lists of unfamiliar names scattered here, there and everywhere. As a matter of fact, these lists are interesting for Bible scholars, not least because of the differences to be found by careful reading and close comparison. It doesn't take an expert, though, to see that the family tree of Jesus as reported by Luke is different from the one Matthew gives in his gospel.

Actually, Matthew is better than Luke for what I am trying to say in this book - I'm underlining the good news that Jesus comes for the outcast and the outsider. The list as given by Matthew famously includes four women and each of them is either a foreigner to Israel or has a slightly unconventional story attached to her in the Old Testament.

An important general point can be made from both genealogies, though: Jesus is human. Unlike some Greek god, he has a list of human ancestors. Even though we rightly stress his birth of the Virgin Mary and the role of the Holy Spirit in this, we equally underline his likeness to us in his humanity and his ordinariness. He is firmly rooted in a Jewish family, but Matthew goes further and traces his ancestry back beyond Abraham, the father of faith, to Adam. The general point to be made is that Jesus is like us, whoever we are (unless in some far future, unearthly aliens are reading this - but that's another story altogether).

William Barclay was a Scottish writer, broadcaster and lecturer on the Bible and he finds material to go even further than this when he writes about the genealogies. It's a bit speculative but his points are well made and are useful to me daily, so I have no hesitation in sharing them here and acknowledging where I found them. Barclay notices that Jesus began his ministry when he was about thirty and rightly asks whether Jesus was not eager to set about his task as Saviour of the World with all the vigour of youth at, say twenty. When I went off to train for Baptist ministry in London I remember my despair at realising I'd be all of thirty when I got out - until someone pointed out to me that thirty is a very scriptural age to start one's life work. None better, in fact. It was the age Jesus began to minister in public.

That Joseph, the earthly father of Jesus, died young and that Jesus had to support his family is Barclay's assumption. Well, we do know from the gospels that Jesus had younger brothers and sisters and that he was taunted with the contemporary stigma of illegitimacy and was sometimes known as 'the son of Mary'. It's a leap of the imagination to suppose as Barclay does that Jesus was the breadwinner of the family but it so happens that I'm ready to jump.

Many of us who want to 'serve God' have had to come to understand that family obligations are part of the deal. I remember when I was a child in Wales being expected to collect money in Sunday School to help fund missionary work overseas so I was dismissive of those who told me when I went abroad myself that I should have been more understanding of the feelings of my parents. After all, I was going to save the world. I think differently today. Jesus tells us that we can only be trusted with great responsibilities if we have been faithful in the small duties. If I were asked to be a member of an interviewing board, as well as asking about family responsibilities, I'd ask any candidate for ministerial training if they know where the vacuum cleaner is kept in their church and if their name is on the rota to wield it.

One of the most uncomfortable feelings in life is being lectured by a much younger and less experienced person, perhaps from a pulpit, on how to live. Mark Twain tells us, quite ruefully, that wisdom comes with the passing of time when he says, 'When I was a boy of 14, my father was so ignorant I could hardly stand to have the old man around but when I got to be 21 I was astonished at how much the old man had learned in seven years.' Jesus is the Teacher of the world as well as the Saviour of the world and it seems to me that you need experience and credibility to take on that role. The workplace is a good place to learn that.

Now that I am self-employed myself, I love the imaginative examples Barclay gives of how Jesus may have won his spurs as a credible teacher. He talks about the haunting insecurity of the life of the self-employed craftsman forever wondering whether enough work will come in. There are days' wages lost to family ill health. There are bad-tempered and critical customers and those who are slow to cough up and settle their debts. I particularly identify with what Barclay says about first-class work undertaken on the cheap or even free for those who have difficulty in paying, because I'm ready to do that myself as long as people don't shout too loudly about my special rates.

This is all speculation, but it is speculation in the right direction if it helps us to realise that Jesus understands us and loves us from the inside and not as a cold observer because any way we can come to understand that Jesus is on our side as we struggle is good. Barclay puts it this way: 'It is the glory of the Incarnation that we face no problem of life and living which Jesus did not also face.' I like to think that the 'hidden years' were when Jesus came to see that God sides with the underdog and the excluded. Luke is so faithful in portraying that aspect of the ministry of Jesus that I know that somehow or another he learned that lesson very thoroughly as he grew and the grace of God was upon him.

Go and teach your granny (Luke 4:14-30)

In his home synagogue in Nazareth those in charge handed Jesus the scroll of the prophet Isaiah and asked him to teach from it. You or I would have turned straight to chapter 53 and used it to foretell the cross and resurrection but Jesus decides to talk instead about chapter 61 with its good news for prisoners, for the blind, the poor and the oppressed.

Before I went to London to train for Baptist ministry in 1985 I was already preaching twice most Sundays alongside the day job as a French teacher and I often talked about this part of Luke. Using it as a pretext, I spent a lot of time and energy trying to establish a link between healing in the time of Jesus and healing today because the Signs and Wonders movement was high on the agenda in those days. However, as I reread it now, I see there's not much about that aspect of the ministry of Jesus here at all but instead there is a huge emphasis on people on the margins and who find themselves strangers to a sense of God's love. The rest of the gospel shows the practical outworking of that emphasis in act and story.

As well as wrongly focussing on physical healing, I somehow managed to spiritualise the message of Jesus too much and was too ready to see the blind and the prisoner as those who have not yet responded to the Christian gospel. This interpretation can be included, of course, but I know now that everything should be in the right place and in due proportion.

Jesus stops reading Isaiah 61 just before it talks about the Day of Judgement of God. Instead of going on, he rolls up the scroll and proclaims that today is the Day of Salvation. So far, so good: something new has come into the world with Jesus. I obviously didn't understand the rest of the passage, though, and all I can remember from those times is thinking, 'Oh, they get a bit irritated with Jesus, they run him out of town and try to throw him off a cliff! I wonder why?' This was my thinking in those days: I'd managed to get the Christian gospel of cross and resurrection out of the passage so why go any further?

That's how I thought in those days and when you are young you often can't be doing with getting background knowledge about a scripture passage, but that's exactly what's needed to understand the dramatic reaction of the crowd. Take that cliff just outside Nazareth they wanted to throw Jesus from: you could see the whole world from up there, not in a literal way but figuratively. In one direction you could look down to the Old Testament lands and think about all the people who made that history - Abraham, Isaac and Jacob, the judges and kings and prophets. If you turned around you could see in imagination the rest of the world with all those dreadful, pagan gentiles.

In the synagogue, it becomes clear that the people in the crowd know that they want Jesus to affirm a local view of the God of Israel, a cosy, inward-looking, domesticated god. What Jesus wants to do, though, is to fulfil the Old Testament and go beyond it. To do that he talks about two characters he would have thought deeply about up on the mountain as he looked towards the Bible lands - Elijah and Elisha.

These two non-writing prophets were already a little bit controversial because they were operating in the northern part of the divided kingdom when all the holy action was down south near Jerusalem. Worse still, some of their most famous exploits were associated with people outside Judaism. A poor widow sheltered Elijah in Sidon during a famine and a feeding miracle and a resurrection from the dead took place. As for Elisha, he was used by God to heal a leper called Naaman who was the captain of the enemy forces fighting against Israel. Jesus compares himself with Elijah and Elisha and by doing so declares that his vision is worldwide and towards outsiders.

When we read the Bible, often our problem is not so much understanding what it says as finding a way of allowing ourselves to be struck by it with the force it originally had. Jesus found a way of sharing the Bible with the synagogue congregation that struck them so powerfully that they tried to strike back and kill him. I suppose to reproduce the power of what he said and the violence of the reaction, you would have to go into the middle of the most conflictual and controversial situation you can think of today, preferably a religious spat, and announce that God loves both sides equally. Like Martin Luther King with his vision of racial equality, Jesus had been up on the mountain and he had seen God's love for the people of the Bible to the south and for the unknown millions elsewhere. And his vision had made him bold.

This is easily said and it's fairly easy to make a list and sound resonantly impressive while making it. That's rhetoric for you. God loves Republican and Democrat, Labour and Tory; his love is for refugee and rejecter; no Palestinian, Syrian or Isis militant is beyond his love; Buddhist, Muslim and Hindu are known to him; 'red and yellow, black and white, all are precious in his sight'.

But what about that person you hate? God doesn't hate that person: God loves them. Somebody hates you, too but don't worry, God loves you as well.

Living for the city (Luke 5:1-11)

I was helping my daughter move house from one side of London to the other a couple of summers ago and I made the most of it by spending a week in the city. I had a real culture overdose, going to the theatre four times and twice to the cinema, hearing Mahler at the Albert Hall, browsing in the National Gallery and the British Museum. I lived in the capital during the 1980s while training to be a Baptist minister but more than ever this time I felt at the heart of national life and I asked myself why anyone would choose to be anywhere else. I know that kind of thinking is a problem for other parts of Britain, not least for our national economic life, but London is a remarkable place all the same.

It occurred to me that if you were aiming to start a new movement, maybe a political party or a religious group, this is where you would start. Once you were there, you could look around for the most influential people and try to bring in the elite opinion makers. Even if you did start your organisation out in the sticks, you'd have to go to London at some point and make your mark there. Jesus was faced with the same phenomenon with regard to Jerusalem. He even said in the course of his ministry, when faced with murderous opposition, that it was not right for a prophet to die anywhere else and eventually it was in the capital city that the work of salvation was 'determined dared and done' by this outsider from the north.

John's gospel seems to assume that all I've been saying so far about the magnetic pull of the big city is true and the writer shows Jesus several times in Jerusalem during the course of his ministry but the other gospels seem to tell a different story. Luke portrays a Jesus who has time for backwaters and the losers who live in them. When he comes to put together his first team of disciples he does it up north, as far from Jerusalem as you could get and still stay in the Holy Land.

Even according to Luke, Jesus had been to Jerusalem, probably many times for national festivals, and he could have done important work there from the start but he chose to lay the foundations of his movement far away from the national centre instead. Similarly, even though there were important people and religious experts in the crowd that began to follow him around and across the Sea of Galilee, he didn't choose these members of the elite to be his closest associates. Instead, he called Peter and his brothers from their fishing nets - a bunch of blunt northerners - and used them to overturn the powerful establishment, starting in Jerusalem and from there to the ends of the earth.

Why Peter? Here are some suggestions in no particular order. Peter is a sceptic and even though he is prepared to voice his doubts that the advice of Jesus about where and when to cast his nets can be trusted, he obeys Jesus all the same. There is only one expert on fishing in the boat, and it's not Jesus, but Peter recognises a kind of authority in the Lord that makes him push the boat out all the same. There is a basic trust there that Jesus can use. Next, when faced even at this early stage with the power and personality of Jesus, Peter is acutely aware of his failings and his need of a saviour. There's an item in Bach's St Matthew Passion that is sung just after the description of Peter's denial of Jesus and just before the cross. It isn't sung by Peter himself but by a singer who might be said to represent you and me, meditating on our own frailty. The accompanying violin solo is perfection itself and all the vocal line can do is sketch in a few lines attempting to match it. Jesus doesn't need those who are convinced of their own righteousness but he can work with those who are aware of their weakness. These he can forgive and remake.

Peter is a leader but not in a way that has to dominate - he's always in the lead but his followers are partners and not subjects. The brothers James and John are first his colleagues in fishing and they become his associates in ministry but it's a story about Peter more than a story about them. Later in the gospel we notice that when the disciples are making mistakes, Peter is in the thick of that too and usually leading in an endearingly fallible way but leading all the same.

Often, a radical change in lifestyle is needed to follow Jesus and Peter is ready for that. For instance, we know that Peter was married - there's no other way that I know of to acquire a mother-in-law - and the apostle Paul confirms this in passing later on. He didn't walk out on his marriage but he did change course. He was still able to use his skills as a fisherman as we see when he catches a fish to pay the Temple tax and when he returns to his nets in the immediate crisis after the cross but essentially he has changed direction and is first of all a disciple and an apostle from now on - a 'following man' and a 'sent man'. The rest of his career shows that despite stumbling falls and foolish misunderstandings and stinging rebukes from another deeply flawed man, namely the apostle Paul, he kept following and kept leading.

Cut to thirty years after the cross and the resurrection and God has chosen the apostle Paul to follow the frustrating strategy of going to the big cities and trying to influence the elite before turning to ordinary people instead. When he got to the centres of population and influence, though, he was repeatedly thrown out of the synagogue, ending up working with the humble to further the cause of Christ: 'Brothers and sisters,' he wrote, 'think of what you were when you were called. Not many of you were wise by human standards; not many were influential; not many were of noble birth. But God chose the foolish things of the world to shame the wise; God chose the weak things of the world to shame the strong. God chose the lowly things of this world and the despised things - and the things that are not - to nullify the things that are.'

Unclean, unclean (Luke 5:12-16)

Cancer, Covid-19, Aids, Ebola - the fight against these diseases goes on and many dedicated people are continuing to study how they are spread, how to contain them and how to help those who fall victim to them. In the meantime, as far as the infectious ones are concerned, people who are thought to have had contact with them are often put in quarantine while sick people are put in sterile rooms if these ideal conditions are available. In Bible times, and in fact in many parts of the world today, it is the same with the often disfiguring disease of leprosy. It has been the same throughout history with its tales of isolated colonies and the ringing of a bell along with the shout of 'unclean' to warn of the approach of a leper or a group of these unfortunate folk.

For people living in the world of Luke's gospel, leprosy was to be feared for another reason - to be a leper made you ritually unclean: as an individual, the disease was thought to shut you out from God and it certainly meant that the life-giving community of faith was closed to you. These exclusions were even wider than a clinical judgement of leprosy. In the Old Testament there is a large section all about the description and diagnosis of 'leprosy' in people, clothes and even housing while there's an equally extensive passage about how to become ritually clean again even after you'd been medically cured. It might well involve destruction of the buildings and garments involved.

So, on top of the danger and the embarrassment of leprosy itself, there was huge inconvenience involved in contact with the scourge, meaning that no one would ever even think of touching a leper. Worse still, there was fear and loathing mingled with the pity people felt towards lepers. There was often self-loathing, too in the groups of lepers and maybe anger against God for allowing the scourge to fall. Luke makes it clear that by touching a leper with the hand of blessing Jesus broke a strict medical taboo and a stern and inflexible religious prohibition at the same time.

This healing miracle was obviously an interesting story for the early Christians because, unlike many incidents, it's in all three of what we call the synoptic gospels - Matthew, Mark and Luke. For us, it's fascinating because it gives us an insight into why we have four gospels in the first place because in each of the three synoptic gospels it's used in a different way. If we read all three gospels together, they give us a fully-rounded picture of Jesus and his ministry.

In Matthew's gospel this miracle marks the beginning of a new section after the Sermon on the Mount and not much more needs to be said than that because it's told baldly without making any particular point: this cleansing simply introduces a new section with a number of healings, the call of Matthew Levi to be a follower of Jesus and then the sending out on mission of the band of disciples.

In Mark's gospel it has much more importance - it shows the mastery of Jesus over sickness as one among a series of events showing his control in a variety of areas. In this section he calms the storm, feeds the crowd, walks on water and raises the dead: he has authority over death, nature, need and sickness. Mark also includes a hugely important single word when we are told that Jesus is either angry or full of compassion when faced with the stark fact of leprosy. The compassionate response we can easily understand but we need to think hard about why Jesus might be angry about sickness. If we do think about it, there are great results, though. Jesus is angry that the world is not as it should be. He is not angry because an unclean man has approached him but because of the condition this poor sufferer who bears the image of God is in. It's helpful to know as you go through life with its many challenges that God is well disposed towards you but not happy at situations you may have to face.

As far as Luke is concerned, the cleansing of the leper illustrates his favourite theme of Jesus including excluded people and letting the stranger in. Here, he tackles the plight of those excluded from the community of Judaism because of leprosy. The story itself is quickly told - the leper uses a hugely symbolic word in asking Jesus for help. The Greek term used for what he wants to happen is not just about healing but about restoring ritual purity. It's about being able to meet God again. Jesus uses the same word right back and tells the leper, 'be clean ritually'. He touches the unclean man who can then go to the priest for the battery of tests to confirm that a wonderful change has taken place.

Jesus tells the leper not to share his story but in a society of gossip and sensationalism it is impossible to keep secret such a dramatic tale of sudden restoration. The resulting publicity means that Jesus is unable to go discreetly about his business but he is able to do one surprising, indeed shocking thing. He is able to pray. That is astonishing, because it shows that the Lord has not been made ritually unclean in spite of touching a leper.

Mark Twain famously said that he was more uncomfortable about the obvious lessons he did understand in Christianity than about the things that were beyond his comprehension. There are several obvious lessons to learn from the story of the cleansing of the leper as Luke tells it and they benefit from being declared simply and without further comment:

When everybody hates and excludes us, Jesus is still prepared to reach out and touch us to make us whole again. When we hate ourselves and can't think why anybody would want to know us, Jesus still wants to know us. When we assume that we are unclean in the eyes of God, Jesus still wants to bring us back into communion with our maker. When we hate or fear someone else, we should remember that Jesus touches them and includes them in the same way that he does for us.

Enormous flakes of dandruff (Luke 5:17-26)

When I was in London I went looking for the site of C.H. Spurgeon's first chapel building in the capital, just south of the river in Southwark and round the corner from the modern reconstruction of Shakespeare's Globe theatre. In the middle of the nineteenth century, it was a dreadful area and the New Park Street Chapel for all its illustrious history had a vinegar factory and breweries as near neighbours. Even I remember something of the shambles this part of the city used to be, because as recently as the 1980s before the current redevelopment you'd look out over disused red-brick factories as your train drew out of London Bridge station and you could easily imagine you were in a Dickens novel even as late as that. The Elephant and Castle area where Spurgeon's Tabernacle was eventually built wasn't a great district but it was definitely a step higher than New Park Street.

Spurgeon began his remarkable ministry here in the 1854 at the age of nineteen. One of his first summers was a hot one and some people in the crowds thronging to hear the teenage prodigy were fainting in the heat. The problem came up for discussion by the deacons but they could reach no decision. The problem was solved temporarily when some unknown person smashed some of the windows at night. Indicating his walking cane, the young preacher said, 'The hand that did the deed has walked with this stick,' or words to that effect.

Early in the ministry of Jesus up north near the Sea of Galilee, he is teaching in a house and a sizeable crowd has squeezed into the cramped dwelling. Suddenly, people are distracted by an insistent knocking coming from above and then pieces of plaster begin settling on the listeners' heads and shoulders, like enormous flakes of dandruff. Then, a gentleman appears - I'll call him Fred - he is lowered in by four straining people bearing the dead weight of a paralysed man. Jesus tells Fred his sins are forgiven. There's a row. Fred walks out under his own steam. The story is simply told.

This is another tale that suggests a background of exclusion and I say this for two reasons. First, if a disabled person wants to attend an event, usually people let them through and make room near the front. This doesn't happen here. Second, I think there's a clue in what Jesus says when he boldly declares, 'Your sins are forgiven.'

I wonder why Jesus says that - he doesn't usually express himself in this way when he is helping or healing. My thoughts run along these lines: often, when some great misfortune occurs, people are quick to identify or even invent some terrible sin that can be held to have caused the calamity. In fact, even the disciples in John's gospel speculate in this way about a man born blind. That type of thinking quickly begins to form part of the definition of a person and pretty soon they themselves start to assume the assessment is true and start to carry it around as a cumbersome and disabling part of their personality.

So, my suggestion is that Fred is being lowered down into the middle of a crowd who look up and see not Fred the person but notorious Fred the infamous sinner. The way I see it, this is why Jesus encourages him with a word about forgiveness in a way that he doesn't usually do.

There is uproar in the crowd at what Jesus says because, very obviously indeed, only God can forgive sins. If you or I started going around telling fairly random people that they are forgiven, first of all they will be angry that you called them a sinner in the first place and then, when they've got over that and you are licking your wounds, they will remember to point out that only God can say that kind of thing anyway.

So, Jesus poses one of his wonderful, enigmatic questions when he asks which is easier, to speak forgiveness or to heal someone who can't walk. It's a marvellous question because it's obviously very easy indeed to talk about forgiveness from God but it's quite impossible to bring it about by human means. Everybody has heard someone say, 'I forgive you' while knowing all too well that the grudge remains for future reference. So, to speak authentically about forgiveness is very hard indeed while, as for healing by a word, it is nearly always out of the question. Healing and forgiveness are both hard things and Jesus heals to show he has God's authority to forgive.

I can't heal people. Only God can do that. Obviously, I can pray for people and even pray for healing and sometimes things happen but often they are ambiguous. I'm happy to pray with anyone at any time for any illness but can give no guarantees except to say that God always hears our prayers. On the other hand, I can say to people, 'your sins are forgiven' and they can go away free of that burden. That may sound very arrogant but Jesus has given that power to us not in ourselves but in the gospel. of Christ. The apostle John gives a clear enough message 'if we confess our sins, God is faithful and just to forgive them'. As a Protestant, I don't much advocate confession to another person as a necessity, although from a human point of view that can help a lot - instead, I tell people to have dealings with God on the basis of the finished work of Christ.

There is one other tiny detail I want to finish with: there are four people up on the earthen roof scrabbling through it and lowering the paralytic precariously down. As Jesus looks up, according to Luke, he sees not the faith of the paralytic but the faith of all of them together. Sometimes, maybe most of the time, we are too weak to have much faith but the faith of others helps us. Our common faith is a very precious thing: the apostle Paul tells us to bear one another's burdens. Maybe we can allow others to carry us into the Christian community for inclusion or maybe for the moment our faith is strong enough to get some other people together and carry someone else.

The happy company (Luke 5:27-32)

Today, we have the luxury of being able to contemplate the Church in all its breadth and diversity: one way or another it includes about a third of humanity with over two billion adherents in over forty thousand denominations, varying in name, emphasis and structure. It has quite a bit of age, too. It's a success story, but how did we get here?

Only Matthew tells us that building the Church was what Jesus had in mind but that gospel states Jesus's aims strongly and tells us that they will not be frustrated whatever opposition they may face. In Luke's gospel there is a lot of mileage in the idea that Jesus is founding a new Israel with twelve founding fathers and there are quite a few parts of the gospel where the language and ideas are meant to make us think of Jesus as a new Moses, leading a new Exodus.

The original twelve founding fathers of Israel, the sons of Jacob, were an uninspiring bunch of people as the book of Genesis makes clear - they cynically sold their own brother into slavery and that was the least of it if you dig a little deeper into the anecdotes about them. You might think that Jesus would do a better job the second time around but as far as his choice of helpers goes, he could hardly have made a worse start in his new enterprise. There is a famous little text that has been around for a long, long time but even now there's still a chance that someone reading this may not have heard of it and anyway it is worth looking at again, especially if you are feeling that you are weak yourself or that your church is going nowhere at this stage of the Great Outworking of the purpose of Jesus. If anyone knows who originally wrote it, I'd love to know.

MEMO TO: JESUS, SON OF JOSEPH, WOODCRAFTER, CARPENTER SHOP, NAZARETH FROM: JORDAN MANAGEMENT CONSULTANTS, JERUSALEM

Dear Sir:

Thank you for submitting the resumes of the 12 men you have picked for management positions in your new organization. All of them have now taken our battery of tests; we have not only run the results through our computer, but also arranged personal interviews for each of them with our psychologist and vocational aptitude consultant. It is the staff opinion that most of your nominees are lacking in background, education, and vocational aptitude for the type of enterprise you are undertaking. They do not have the team concept. We would recommend that you continue your search for persons of experience in managerial ability and proven capability. Simon Peter is

emotionally unstable and given to fits of temper. Andrew has absolutely no qualities of leadership. The two brothers, James and John, the sons of Zebedee, place personal interest above company loyalty. Thomas demonstrates a questioning attitude that would tend to undermine morale. We feel that it is our duty to tell you that Matthew has been blacklisted by the Greater Jerusalem Better Business Bureau. James, the son of Alphaeus, and Thaddaeus definitely have radical leanings, and they both registered a high score on the manic depressive scale. One of the candidates, however, shows great potential. He is a man of ability and resourcefulness, meets people well, has a keen business mind and has contacts in high places. He is highly motivated, ambitious, and responsible. We recommend Judas Iscariot as your controller and right-hand man. All of the other profiles are self-explanatory. We wish you every success in your new venture.
Sincerely yours, Jordan Management Consultants

If you were feeling charitable you might say that Jesus saw potential in this first group of disciples but if you didn't know that these people were behind a massive global concern with two millennia of history you'd say it just shows poor judgement. I want to look at the disciples as a whole later on but just for now I'll concentrate on one of the chosen, Levi or Matthew.

My theme in 'Luke, Stranger' is exclusion and, as he first appears, Matthew Levi is a great example of this. As soon as Jesus sets foot in this tax collector's house there's a huge outcry from religious people and it's clear that the only people who would associate with a man like him were other tax collectors and their limited circle of friends and associates. After all, such men were usually traitors in the pay of the occupying army who would set a financial target for a given area and then set about reaching it by any means, with enough left over to pay a personal wage. They were involved in imposing poll taxes, taxes on goods and loan sharking. They were proverbial for their wealth obtained by dishonest means and if they were unwelcome in the synagogue, well, so be it. We all have to earn a living.

So why does Jesus go into Matthew's house? Because only sick people need a doctor and only those on the outside need to come in. Jesus states and demonstrates that cheats and thieves need God as much as religious people - not more, you notice - and that they deserve a chance to respond to the call of their maker the same as anyone else does.

If that's why Jesus goes into Matthew Levi's house, we also need to know why a pariah like Matthew decides to follow Jesus and become one of his disciples. After all, what could be better than financial security no matter how it has been obtained? There are many people today in many settings who would love to be able to achieve such independence but have little chance of ever doing so.

Well, if you are excluded, you long above all to be in a group of people and if the only people who will be seen with you are frauds and hucksters, you want to be surrounded by just a few folks who are not in that category. The group around Jesus is a very attractive one. This couldn't be said about John the Baptist's group with its asceticism or even about the broader Judaism of the time characterised on one side by rules and regulations and on the other by uneasy collaboration with the Romans. Jesus said his group was more like a wedding reception or, even better than that, like bride and groom united in intimacy and joy. Of course, he knows that the Cross is coming and he will talk about it with increasing urgency later in the gospel as he goes up to Jerusalem but for now the Church, if we can already call it that, is a warm, welcoming and affirming group of people. William Barclay, the Scottish writer, broadcaster and lecturer calls it The Happy Company.

And then there's the appeal of Jesus himself. He had a knack of turning people against him to the point that they felt they had no option but to crucify him but not before they'd admitted that they'd never heard or seen anyone like him and not before he'd given them a chance to respond in ways other than by suspicion and hate.

So, if Jesus turned to you personally and told you to follow him, as he did to Matthew Levi, you did so. Unlike the volatile crowds, you followed him almost to the cross before you felt you had to save your own skin. Then, after his rising from the dead you followed him again, this time till your own death and even beyond. However badly you let him down, you kept on being drawn and when you stumbled you picked up the pieces and just kept going. The Calvinists talk about an 'irresistible call' and a 'final perseverance'. A man like Matthew Levi shows us what those dry, dusty doctrinal terms mean in practice. Even an excluded person man like Matthew could be welcomed in The Happy Company an then keep on going till the end.

Frantic Leisure (Luke 6:20-26)
Miguel D. Lewis said that, 'Capitalism is religion. Banks are churches. Bankers are priests. Wealth is heaven. Poverty is hell. Rich people are saints. Poor people are sinners. Commodities are blessings. Money is God.'

If this is true, then the high priests of the religion in question are the fewer than a hundred people in the world who own as much as billions of the poorest put together. Life expectancy, conditions of life and opportunities for improvement follow the money. Even in the UK - a country with a long history of excellent free education - I am often told in conversation that if parents want to provide their children with a really good chance in life, they must pay for a better school. Once upon a time you had to put aside savings for your daughter's wedding but now you have to save up to pay for her internship as well. Actually, given the extent of inequality, you may not have to save and if you have enough for one, you probably have enough for the other and maybe a start on the property ladder into the bargain.

We at the bottom are subjected to a lot of messages designed to train us to be disciples of these high priests and to aspire to their conditions of life, most of us just about managing to hold a place in one of the richest countries on earth. But, there is discontent up there in the clouds: my observation suggests that unlimited money and clocks full of free time often lead to a despairing emptiness filled with increasingly frantic leisure activities.

The whole religion is fake and Jesus doesn't hesitate to reverses its standards. Listening to him can help us to overthrow the tables in the temple even today.

Every year at the War Memorial in our village, I used to read the Beatitudes from Matthew's gospel as part of the Remembrance Day ceremony. At times like that when we remember conflict, we want to know that the world can be different. In Luke's gospel, there seems to be something wrong with the Beatitudes. In Matthew, Jesus says, 'Blessed are the poor in spirit' and 'Blessed are those who hunger and thirst after righteousness' but in Luke he says, 'Blessed are you poor people' and 'Blessed are you hungry folk.' Not only so, but in Luke Jesus adds 'Woe to you rich' and 'Woe to you who are well fed.' Luke somehow manages to be more terse and more expansive at the same time.

Maybe Jesus gave similar teaching in different forms in different places - after all, The Sermon on the Mount in Matthew becomes the Sermon on the Plain in Luke. I think there may be some mileage in the fact that Matthew was Jewish and coming from a tradition of Midrash which involves giving interpretative additions to an authoritative text. So, it's possible to suggest that Matthew gives the spiritual interpretation behind the brass tacks of Jesus's sayings found in Luke.

You could summarise Matthew like this: Blessed are those who are dissatisfied with the current way of things because God will satisfy them spiritually either now or at some time in the future.

Luke is more down to earth than that and he is concerned all the way through his gospel with those who are not invited to a top table groaning under the weight of the good things of life. The blunt teaching is in Luke and one valuable principle of interpretation where there are questions about a text says that we should prefer the trickier version simply because it is so thorny and so hard to accept.

As for what he says, we need to remember Jesus is speaking in front of a large crowd but looking at his twelve new disciples, none of whom has influence in worldly terms. I suppose if you started a new business from scratch you might begin by talking with the first employees about the core values of the organisation - what kind of values the company has and what kinds of rewards the workers can expect. What Jesus shares is quite a long mission statement but it qualifies as one, all the same:

'Blessed are you who are poor,
for yours is the kingdom of God.
Blessed are you who hunger now,
for you will be satisfied.
Blessed are you who weep now,
for you will laugh.
Blessed are you when people hate you,
when they exclude you and insult you
and reject your name as evil,
because of the Son of Man.
Rejoice in that day and leap for joy, because great is your reward in heaven. For that is how their ancestors treated the prophets.
But woe to you who are rich,
for you have already received your comfort.
Woe to you who are well fed now,
for you will go hungry.

Woe to you who laugh now,
for you will mourn and weep.
Woe to you when everyone speaks well of you,
for that is how their ancestors treated the false prophets.'

The job description of the follower of Jesus as represented by these twelve disciples in that open-air boardroom is to identify with the billions in their masses and not the tiny proportion of individuals. George Orwell said of the one per cent, 'Apparently nothing will ever teach these people that the other 99% of the population exist.' It is the job of the disciple to notice the existence of the 99%, to identify with them and plead their cause. To identify with the poorest in the country and with the poorest in the world - the 4am cleaners and carers on the minimum wage in the UK and those who carry dirty water several miles to survive on other continents.

As for rich people, 'you have already received your comfort'. You are likely to be reliant on what has been amassed and have already taken whatever joy it can give. Why should God help with his kingdom resources those who have no need of them? I say, 'likely', because even though Jesus is critical of riches to an extent that the disciples are shocked, even though the New Testament includes material about money that suggests we should avoid excess of it as we would avoid the mythical Shirt of Nessus, Jesus does make a concession. Even though you'll never get a camel through the eye of a needle, no matter how hard you try, with God even the rich can be saved.

Everybody reading 'Luke, Stranger' will know that it's not possible to live without food or money or joy or social acceptance. Welcome to the Bible which is a world of false oppositions and exaggerated dichotomies to make a point. After all, it's a world where you have to hate your parents to follow Jesus. It seems to me that Jesus is saying with great force that his disciples must be single-minded in identifying with the poor. The Beatitudes in Luke are saying that God must be the main thing, not money. God must be the focus for the disciples, not food. God must be taken seriously and not treated with levity or as of secondary importance. God must be followed even if it means an end to dreams of popularity.

Strange meeting (Luke 6:27-36)
You've already met an American couple called Chuck and Cathy Powers I knew when we were together helping the homeless in Toulouse in the South of France. Shortly after I came back to Wales in 2002 they moved up north near Boulogne and Calais to work with the family of one of these unfortunate people and from time to time I go across and visit them, especially now they are going back and forth to the refugee camps to bring support to these other poor victims of these

turbulent times. It's just about possible to drive across for the weekend with a car full of clothes and food for the Calais Jungle.

In Chuck and Cathy's little town of Desvres I must have passed the local cemetery dozens of times on my way to the baker's for my morning croissants and I had already noticed the plaque by the entrance saying 'Commonwealth War Graves' - in fact, once I did go in and had a look around but couldn't find anything. Last time I was there, what with the commemorations of the centenary of World War One, I decided to try a bit harder so I went to find the attendant and asked where I should look. He was very helpful and showed me the four final resting places, not in a row as I'd imagined but scattered around the place.

One of the fallen was called William Davies and as Davies is a Welsh name I was curious to learn more about how this young man of twenty years of age came to be here so many miles from the front line in 1917. So, I went on the internet and found out he was from Bedwellty. That made things even more interesting because my home town, Abertillery, used to be in the administrative district known as Bedwellty. I put all the details I had on an internet site concerned with Monmouthshire local history and, sure enough, more information came back quickly. People back home told me this soldier was from Argoed, just over the mountain from where I grew up. I put flowers on the grave and took a picture that I showed to my elderly neighbour when I came back. She is from Argoed and her maiden name was Davies but it's not the same branch of the family so the trail goes cold here.

I've thought a lot about this incident and even shared about it in a Quaker meeting I attended - a first for me. I feel the experience of meeting a local boy so far from home has taught me something important about how we are all connected. The fact that I could find out so much information through the internet even when abroad suggests to me that when we work together we can do so much more than when we choose to go it alone.

Of course, it's easy to talk about connection when it reveals links with people we like, with friends and family, with compatriots, or people with similar interests and background but Jesus goes further than this and tells us to pray not only for those we like but even for our enemies. In fact, maybe we should pray especially for our enemies. After all, as Jesus says, it's no credit to us if we love those who love us but if we love those opposed to us and do good to them, we are like God who makes his sun shine on good people and bad people alike.

I heard a performance of Benjamin Britten's 'War Requiem' recently and this piece inspired by World War Two ends with a setting of Wilfred Owen's poem about connectedness between a soldier and his killer - 'Strange Meeting', it's called. But it's a connection in futility and in the destruction of life itself which should be cherished and nurtured. 'I am the enemy you killed, my friend'. Britten's masterpiece is meant to encourage listeners to use greater determination to break down walls and build bridges with the stones.

It's obvious that Christians have that kind of connection with other believers and there are many ways we can give expression to it but this link also extends to all humanity and we must not try to deny it or free ourselves of its obligations. It seems to me that although we believe we belong to a new humanity being born, we still belong to the old one. It seems to me that we are looking at the apostle Paul's famous struggle between the old man of the flesh and the new man of the Spirit only on a larger stage that goes far beyond the individual. We are to pray for all, work for peace with all and love all with no exceptions unless we want to stop being like God whose 'common grace' to all humankind we are to imitate without limit.

Christians have another connectedness apart from this link with humanity as a whole and maybe it is more important still than the bond of common grace we share with all humankind. I have sometimes heard it said that the famous passage in Matthew's gospel where Jesus talks about a separation between the sheep and the goats is talking about a judgement based on how we act towards our fellow Christians when we see they are in need. I'm not sure about that, because it seems to me that nothing in our faith frees us from an obligation to respond to the suffering of humanity as a whole.

All the same, there is a connection with follow Christians that is of a different kind: as followers of Christ we celebrate the fact that we have somehow and for some reason that escapes us for the moment - certainly there is nothing in us to deserve it - been called to a community of worship. The book of Revelation portrays a great crowd of people just like us who have come out of the great tribulation of life and the furnace of persecution. It describes them as having washed their garments in the blood of the lamb and we hear their songs of praise and in fact we let those songs nourish our own life of worship as we join in with them.

So, whatever we conclude about the extent of common grace and our responsibility to help those in trouble with whom we don't share an explicitly Christian connection, this strand of the Bible describes people like us who have received a special grace or a saving grace. 'Saviour if of Zion's city I though grace a member am,' wrote the former slave trader John Newton, 'let the world deride or pity, I will glory in thy name.' Whatever the result of the cosmic struggles for the world at large and whatever the final extent of the Church when it reaches its final convert, we worship with the church in the here and now whether on earth or in the nearer presence of God.

We are connected with every person and group in the world who belongs to that great throng in our generation: we call this the

Church militant. We know it includes Christians like us with our relatively peaceful and untroubled Christian life and with a greater or lesser degree of prosperity but it also includes Christians being harassed and persecuted in Iraq, in China, in Nigeria, in the Ukraine - the list goes on. We are also, incidentally in connection not only with the Church militant but also with what we call the Church triumphant, namely all the Christians who have already made it safely through to the presence of God. It's hard to imagine but given that God dwells in eternity, even Christians yet to be born are connected to us in Him!

The apostle Paul had two magnificent obsessions that come across in all his letters. The first was to preach Christ wherever his name was not yet known and honoured; everyone knows about that aim. The second is less well-known but very prominent nonetheless. I'm talking about his collection for the impoverished Church in Jerusalem which was subject to a famine foretold by prophecy. Almost certainly, Paul saw this collection as an important feature in hastening the return of Christ to make everything right again as it was in the beginning.

We imitate Paul not only when we speak the gospel but also when we seek ways of expressing our connectedness with all Christians and particularly with those who are suffering at the moment and for whom the great tribulation is more than just a theory about the end of the world. We live in times when fellow Christians are very publicly suffering for political reasons but also for their faith alone.

All the same, if I had to choose between helping other Christians and helping without distinction, I think I would say that it's a mistake for our Christian identity to stand in the way of our common humanity and that we should love, pray and serve without distinction and with no limits to our compassion. Christians are suffering right now and we are called to do what we can to help them but our brothers and sisters are not the only ones in trouble and we must help those with no Christian affiliation too. Not only so but while doing all we can to neutralise their evil efforts, we should pray for and love even those who cause the suffering until the end when hardship and tears are no more.

Here is a poem based on what is often known as 'the love chapter', 1 Corinthians 13. It can be sung as a hymn to the beautiful Irish tune Londonderry Air, also known as Danny Boy. Love really is 'The Better Way'. What a breadth of vision that chapter has when it talks about God's love when compared with our own efforts.

If we could speak all tongues of earth and heaven
But have not love our prophecy is vain;
Though every mystery to us is open
All talk of love will be an empty claim.
But love is swift to clear misunderstanding,

Love is not proud, insisting on display
And love is rich in patient understanding:
Grant us, oh Lord of love to seek the better way.

If we should give to others when we prosper
But have not love, we fail the final test
If we should place our substance on the altar
Our sacrifice, if boastful, is not blessed.
For love is clean and clear in its intentions,
Lifts up its face to face the light of day,
Love is pure harmony without pretension:
Grant us, oh Lord of love to find the better way.

If by our faith we make the mountains tremble
But have not love, then nothing do we win:
We are but noisy gongs or clanging cymbals
Condemned to sink to silence in the end.
But love is always faithful in rejoicing,
Lifts up a song of hope that never fails
Love is a choir of perfect blended voices
Grant us, oh Lord of love to choose the better way.

When we were young we fought for worldly glory,

But worldly ways in time all have to die.

We see in part as in a mirror darkly

And wait in hope for love's bright sun to rise.

Faith, hope and love, these three remain our story

But faith and hope will vanish in the day;

As we await love's triumph in the glory

Grant us, oh Lord of love to love the better way.

Faith in Jackboots (Luke 7:1-17)

There was an exercise I had to do when I was studying poetry called 'compare and contrast' - in an exam they used to put two poems side by side and you had to say what was similar and what was different about them. It's a good discipline and I'm glad I did it because it helps you to read closely all the time, whatever you read.

I've begun to notice that in Luke's gospel the miracle stories sometimes occur side by side in pairs. There's the man with leprosy and the paralytic lowered in through the roof. I've said they're both stories about exclusion, one because of sickness and the other because of accusation. Later on, we are told about a centurion's servant and a widow's only child. Because the stories are told together, they can throw light on each other. We can compare and contrast.

The raising of the widow's child is an exemplary gospel

miracle: it ticks all the boxes so well that the Crusaders built a church in the place where it was said to have happened. There are familiar themes to do with God's help for the weak. Because it is a widow getting help from God, we are reminded of the song of Mary at the very beginning of the gospel - a song about God's compassion towards the helpless but we need to remember that this is a theme of the Bible as a whole, not just of this gospel. 'True religion cares for the widow and the orphan' writes James in his letter but when he says this he is not saying anything new but just being a faithful echo of the Old Testament in the Law, the prophets and the stories that are told.

Jesus brings the Kingdom of God into a situation where things have broken down and there is only despair. So often, Jesus tells his disciples, 'Do not be afraid' and here he instructs the widow to stop crying. He touches the coffin and the young man inside is raised from the dead. After the immediate outburst of joy, astonishment and worship, maybe later in the day when they got a chance to reflect on what had happened, everybody in the crowd would have been talking about the prophet Elijah who had similarly raised a widow's son. Luke tells us that the witnesses come to the conclusion that they've seen the work of a great man of God in Jesus.

If I had been writing this gospel, putting the available materials in a coherent order as Luke starts his gospel by telling us he has done, I would have put the healing of the Centurion's servant after this and made some contrasts between the two miracles. As a matter of fact, the military miracle comes first. Yes, there are similarities - there is a healing and compassion shown in a situation of great distress, but you'd expect that in incidents like these. There is a child involved in each but the widow's son is already a young man.

The contrasts between the stories are more striking than the similarities. Most of the people Jesus helps are poor nobodies but this is a Roman centurion. These men are always portrayed favourably in the New Testament - they are always well-respected and reliable people who speak truth, maybe more truth than they could rationally know, as they speak their minds. For instance, the first words of faith when Jesus has died on the cross are from a centurion: 'Truly, this man was the son of God.'

I remember once going out door-knocking with a member of a church in East London. We were to ask the question, 'If you were to die tonight, why would God let you into heaven?' The man with me was explaining how to answer different types of response. He began, 'If you get a "worksy" reply then the person is relying on his own efforts to please God.'

We are used to playing down the importance of good works to please God because our gospel is one of faith but we shouldn't let that emphasis blind us to the fact that God loves good things and kind behaviour whoever is showing it and whenever it is shown. So, the love of the centurion for his *pais* - his child-servant - is underlined in a context where servants, and certainly slaves, were often expendable commodities. The centurion's love for the synagogue is mentioned with approval in a world of suspicion and mutual distrust. This was a man who took God into account in his dealings with his staff and with the subject people. Even if good works do not save people, God loves them all the same and maybe they are a sign that someone is reaching out towards him.

So often in the gospels people come to Jesus in such a lot of trouble that all they can bring by way of explanation sounds like so much doubting, questioning and despair. By contrast, the robust faith of the centurion is remarkable even to Jesus. His is a very fine speech and he makes a good analogy: if an army officer always gets his orders obeyed, so will an order of the Son of God be met with an obedient response. Jesus is often amazed at the lack of faith of his disciples - 'O ye of little faith' is a kind of refrain in the gospel and has passed into the English language as a saying - so, to be amazed by someone's faith is quite exceptional in Jesus. He is amazed by the faith of the centurion.

Jesus is often very tactile - he breaks the bread, he makes a paste of spit and mud and smears it on the blind man's eyes, he put his fingers in a deaf man's ears. Here, though, he heals at a distance and with a word, just as God had created with a word in the beginning of all things. That might encourage us as we pray to remember that neither distance in miles nor in time is an obstacle for him.

What might have shocked people living at the time of Jesus was that he had time for the centurion at all: for all his good works and his fine speech and upstanding character, he was still an occupying soldier. But we see any hint of Jewish exclusivism subverted by Jesus himself, the King of the Jews. Suddenly we remember the Nazareth Manifesto and we remember why they tried to throw Jesus off a cliff. The widow helped by Elijah helped was not a Jew at all, she was 'the widow of Zarephath' in the foreign territory of Sidon.

Then, it all slots into place. These two miracles are together to show us in an exercise of compare and contrast that God is on the side of the insider in Israel and the outsider in uniform alike.

I've been had (Luke 7:18-35)

Imagine that you see the most terrific bargain on the internet - it's a device that'll do all the washing and ironing, take care of any shopping that needs to be done and cook for the family - it'll even do the cleaning and decorate the house! That's such a bargain that you pay out your £200 and arrange to have it delivered. You wait in, because you don't want to get a card telling you to go to Swindon to pick it up and finally the van draws up outside. It's a large, rectangular package. You tear open the box and rip the protective plastic to shreds, only pausing to pop a few bubbles. What a disappointment when it turns out to be a only a mirror - a lovely mirror but a mirror all the same. You've wasted your money and you still have all the chores to do. You didn't read the small print.

Now try to put yourself in the place of John the Baptist. You know you have a call from God because your elderly parents told you about the remarkable circumstances surrounding your birth and that of your cousin and contemporary, Jesus of Nazareth. The Bible verse, 'The child grew and the grace of God was upon him' was written not about Jesus but about you. When you became an adult, you began to call people powerfully back to God by underlining the Law of Moses and its implications. Large crowds gather and come for baptism to show that they are turning back to God and, what's more, your work has an important social dimension as you preach justice and mercy to attentive taxman and the military.

In spite of such a successful ministry, you still remember that your work is only that of a forerunner because you have meditated deeply on the words of the prophet Malachi about the coming of Elijah before the advent of the Messiah. You're not very comfortable with this description because you are humble, so you prefer to be known as The Voice calling out about preparing the way of the Lord. Reflection on the prophecy of Isaiah has revealed that role to you.

Jesus himself comes to be baptised among the thousands of others but, uniquely, God singles him out by the descent of a dove and a voice from heaven echoing your own cry. You have baptised men and women head and shoulders above Jesus for influence in the society and far more becoming in their appearance but this time you know your message has to change, in spite of any preconceptions you may have had about what the Christ would look like. So, you tell your disciples to follow Jesus and for the most part they do just that. As for you, your influence decreases. As your following dwindles, you become vulnerable to attack where before you could rely on the crowds to help you to ignore the disapproval of the establishment.

Now, obviously, because you've already seen a massive revival from God, you expect an even bigger one now that Jesus has been revealed to you. You expect God to act decisively: surely, he will put an end to Roman rule and bring corruption in Church and State to an end with 'the turning of the page and the curtain rising on a New Age' as Bob Dylan put it in his song 'Groom's still waiting at the altar'. You watch attentively but you don't see it. Instead, all you see is Jesus sharing meals with sinful people, touching unclean folk and helping Roman officers. What's more, his rise to prominence has given your enemies the green light to close in on you and when one of the rulers you criticise takes exception to your preaching, you end up in jail. You had a mission and you fulfilled it as best you knew how before handing on the torch but your successor is at ease eating and drinking with the dregs of society.

So, you send a couple of your remaining disciples to bring a message to Jesus asking whether a big mistake has been made and it's time to make a deal with the authorities, get out on bail and start building a following again. The reply from Jesus is cryptic: 'The blind receive sight, the lame walk, those who have leprosy are cleansed, the deaf hear, the dead are raised, and the good news is proclaimed to the poor. Blessed is anyone who does not stumble on account of me.'

You have to search all your knowledge of the Hebrew Scriptures to get an inkling that the power of God is shown above all when he has pity on the weak. Just as that reality begins to dawn on you, your executioners arrive and only by God's grace are you safe with the Lord when you suffer the indignity of having your severed head brought out at to be presented on a platter to Salome at Herod's Banquet.

When I started following Jesus, I expected so much more from God than I ever saw. I remember leaving my teaching job in 1985 and going to London to be trained for Baptist ministry. One of my friends claimed to have a prophecy for me that predicted great things and another asked me how I saw my work panning out. It was the tail end of the time when the preaching campaigns of Billy Graham were still filling football stadiums in Great Britain and it was an optimistic time for my wing of the British church, so I said that I could see myself preaching in front of huge crowds just as the American evangelist did.

It hasn't worked out that way. I remember a pastors' meeting in Bordeaux when as a group of American and British ministers, all of us very capable people, we were licking our wounds after years of serving in the wilderness of south-west France and the suggestive phrase, 'disappointed in our ministry' came up in prayer and seemed all too accurate.

All the same, I've always tried to be attentive to what God has for me and over more than thirty years of ministry I've found satisfaction in listening to hurting people, in serving coffee to the homeless and in bringing food to refugees fleeing conflict in the Middle East in the Calais Jungle. Much of this work has been exhausting and thankless and I've had some serious bouts with depression while the churches I know seem for the most part to have gone on declining while their members, in a buyers' market, make the rounds of the shows on offer and create in some places an illusion of growth. I've found, though, that there is no better feeling than realising someone has chosen to unburden to you - unless it's bringing practical help to someone who is physically hungry. Sometimes I do wonder whether I have really understood God's word and way for me but I continue to hope so.

I wonder what you, as you read this, expected from God when

you began to follow him. Maybe someone rashly promised you that all your problems would be solved and you would obtain not only forgiveness but prosperity. Maybe you started out on the Christian pilgrimage on that basis. That person forgot to tell you there was a cost to be counted and a cross to be carried. Perhaps your road has been rocky and strewn with financial issues, health problems, and bereavements, maybe in tragic circumstances. Nonetheless, the word comes back from Jesus: you've found peace with God; you've found his strength in weakness; you've found grace to help in time of need. We should never forget that in what is often called 'the faith chapter', Hebrews 11, not one of the heroes of faith received the promise during their lifetime. Their call was not only to great faith but to great faithfulness.

Demons (Luke 8:26-39)
Perhaps the most obvious example of all of an excluded outsider in Luke's gospel is this passage about the man living among the tombs. I didn't deal with that incident in the original preaching series I have used for this book. That was because, while I am committed to teaching 'the whole counsel of God', I also believe in letting sleeping dogs lie. In the congregation where I was ministering, for the vast majority of members, the issue of demonic possession does not seem to have any practical interest outside Hollywood while there is always

a tiny number of people who are morbidly excited by such things. I felt it was best not to arouse an unhealthy interest on the one hand and not to encourage an unbalanced world-view on the other. I'm not a coward but I do believe in keeping my powder dry.

Now I am no longer a Baptist minister in any particular church, I feel a certain liberty to speak my mind in a way that may not be helpful when trying to lead Christian people forward in unity. So, let me say that in thirty years of ministry, although I have had to try to help many very severely disturbed people, all but one or two I think can be easily explained in psychiatric terms. Even those isolated and frightening cases I now feel inclined to think of as the most extreme examples I ever saw of trouble of this kind. My mind goes back to Toulouse at about three in the morning and I am going up to the eleventh floor in the lift and the roaring, pulsating music is increasing in volume up there as I get closer and I am trembling in anticipation of what I might find. Maybe I will be thrown from the balcony by this disturbed man?

We see in the passage a wretched man living naked among the tombs and completely out of the reach of society's calming influence, whether by persuasion or force. He meets Jesus with anguish and with an apparently supernatural knowledge of the Lord's name and mission. When challenged, the demons reveal themselves as being many and as having a collective name, Legion. They beg Jesus to send them into a herd of pigs and, when this is done, the poor swine destroy themselves in the lake while the man is restored to his right mind and goes to share the good news of the power of the Christ who has included him once again in God's people.

Luke clearly accepts this story at face value in the terms he describes: a legion of demons has taken control of this man. This need not pose a problem for us because all the Bible authors were writing with a world-view which was limited, in its political and social frame of reference and here in its notions notion of the spiritual world. Incidentally, in for a penny in for a pound, I sometimes wonder whether, rather than trying to pretend by tortuous exegesis that the Bible is not opposed to women in ministry or homosexuality, people shouldn't just recognise these teachings for what they are and say they disagree with the starting point of writers who unquestioningly accepted the presuppositions of their day. I don't expect to be popular for that point of view but it seems far more honest to me than twisting the Bible to make it say what you want it to say.

As far as Jesus himself is concerned, apparently he is operating within the same way of looking at things as Luke. Some will see this as an automatic endorsement of Dr Luke's diagnosis but I question that for two reasons. First, it is often said that Jesus accommodated himself to the level of understanding of his disciples. According to this argument, even though Jesus knew that the problem here was really a psychiatric one, he was prepared to act as though demons were involved. I think there is mileage in this view.

For my part, though (and this is my second reason) I don't see any problem in Jesus himself having an erroneous view in this case. After all, we believe that in Jesus, God limited himself, and to my mind that doesn't rule out his confining himself to the body and mind of a first century Galilean. I am on record as saying that notwithstanding his intimate connection with his heavenly Father, the main way that Jesus learned about his role and mission as Saviour of the World was through the study of scripture and through prayer rather than by direct illumination. The alternative is strange indeed: a baby in a manger who knows about nuclear physics, geology, the symphonies of Beethoven and so on.

In support of the opinion that Luke's world-view is the correct one, some will point to what appear to them convincing examples of demonic possession today, often in parts of the world where Christianity has historically had little influence. Well, first of all, I need to see more evidence: most of what I hear about such possession as well as about widespread physical healing today is second-hand and anecdotal and seems to me to feed superstition more than it does faith.

On the other hand, I must admit to having some respect for the view that maybe a concentration of demonic activity was stirred up by

Jesus's saving ministry and that when the gospel comes to a society for the first time, a similar conflict takes place. This is a working model that has the merit of underlining the power of the Cross both then and now. My preferred view at the moment, though, is that everywhere people manifest their trouble in a way that is expected in their culture and that the apparently miraculous nature of their cure is similarly according to what is expected of them. We must never underestimate people's willingness both consciously and at a subconscious level to conform whether to a supernatural or to a psychiatric model, according to the context.

We may be permitted to have some concern for the pigs and for their owners deprived of their livelihood. I think it would have been irresponsible of Jesus to send any demons there might have been into that herd only for them to be destroyed, even if he wanted to assure the man among the tombs of his deliverance. I doubt very much that demons can drown anyway. I tend to think - and I am not alone in this - that they were distressed by the astonishing commotion taking place and simply ran away.

Once, when I was involved in an evangelistic mission in the east end of London, the work was very hard indeed and the other members of the team began to feel that there was demonic opposition at work and that it was focused on an occult bookshop in the high street of the town where we were working. I was sceptical at the time and wish I had been more outspoken than I was in expressing my view. Maybe I, too, fell under the spell more than I care to admit. Perhaps I was afraid of appearing less spiritually acute than the others claimed to be. What I should have said is that that Christ on the Cross won a victory over any powers that may be and that to have a superstitious dread is surely unworthy of the followers of Jesus. When I am asked to embrace faith in the demonic world as having equal weight with my faith in God, I feel I have to refuse nowadays.

Smile at the storm (Luke 8:40-56)
There's a communion hymn that we used to sing every month in the last church where I served and I love it because it talks more than most songs do these days about those of us who are 'caught in the storm', those 'whose faith is spent' and whose 'hope is bruised and bent.' I used to play the piano in the church services and one month I stopped playing to listen to individual voices in the congregation as they sang it and because I knew many of their stories intimately, I very nearly wept as I remembered what life had thrown at them while I provided whatever support I could as the tempest rose still higher and the billows rolled.

Jesus is asleep in the boat when a deadly storm blows up. He trusts the experienced sailors to keep him safe and there is a trust in God even higher than that, so he doesn't wake up because of fear but because the terrified mariners rouse him. From what they saw him do and heard him say next they learned important lessons: Jesus is able to calm the tempests in life and a typhoon can be faced out with the gift of faith. I don't minimise the ferocity of the howling gales we can face in life - God knows, I really and truly don't - but Jesus can mitigate them and there is a way through to a calmer place.

Safely back on shore, Jesus meets two people caught in the storm of life whose 'hope is bruised and bent'. It is most unusual in the gospels to have one story enclosed within another: it's almost a novelistic approach which means that the stories are sharply contrasting but invite comparison at the same time. Incidentally, Jesus is interrupted on the way to a dramatic healing and his response shows that when we are interrupted, we should not be impatient but consider that the interruption may be a God-given opportunity to help the person we perceive as interrupting the real business of the moment. But I digress.

First to appear on the scene is Jairus the synagogue ruler who is living through an extreme crisis. He has reached the pinnacle of his profession and has all the honours that life in his line of work can afford but they are worthless to him now that his daughter, on the brink of womanhood in this culture, is at the point of death.

Jairus was not too proud to ask for help from someone who had brought trouble to the synagogue. Most of us think we can handle the crises that happen in our lives by ourselves and much of the time and to an extent we can, so we prefer not to ask others to help us unless we really have to because we can no longer rely on our own resources. But there comes a time when we are overwhelmed and our own resources are no longer sufficient. There will come a time to us all when we are beyond any human resources - the valley of the shadow of death. Then, it's necessary to leave behind the self-sufficiency and come to God with our need.

I'm not saying we should wait until there's a crisis before we come to God. It's better to have a consistent walk with him so that when the crisis comes we already know where to turn but it's in our human nature to forget God when things are going well. D.L. Moody, a great American preacher, wisely said that , 'we can stand affliction better than we can prosperity for in prosperity we forget God'.

Whatever his reasons for coming to Jesus, we see that the faith of Jairus was a stubborn one even when from every point of view it was already too late. After all, the wailing women had already stepped in and taken over his home and were already busy making the salmon sandwiches for the wake. It was clearly too late for Jesus to step in, but even when it appears too late, it is still time to pray stubbornly. In this instance, in the midst of ridicule, Jesus does his work and even adds a delightful human detail about food when he tells the mourners to give something to eat to the little girl he has raised from the dead.

Apparently (and many of us have observed this) dying is hard physical work and you need refreshment after it.

In the middle of this story about Jairus is an incident involving a woman who has been ill for 12 years - coincidentally, her illness began at the same time as Jairus's daughter was born. Hers is a different kind of storm: her 'hope is bruised and bent' and her 'heart is tired and sore'. In the words of a great and realistic song by Graham Kendrick, for her, there are, 'nights of doubt and worry where sleep has fled away.' Her hopes have been repeatedly lifted by new doctors and new remedies but again and again those hopes have been dashed and disappointed. Luke leaves out a detail the other gospel writers give us - not only did she not get better, 'instead she got worse'. Luke was a doctor and those in the medical profession don't like to fail, even though, in 100% of cases, they do, in the end.

Like Jairus, this lady has a stubborn faith and even in the male-defined exclusion of the ritual uncleanness connected with her twelve-year flow of blood, she is prepared to reach out for the touch of a tassel on the far fringes of the garment of Jesus. That simple touch is enough to connect with the Lord and for the power to go out of him to heal.

There's a detail I'd never noticed in this incident before reading it the other day. I remember her trembling as she approaches Jesus but I'd never noticed that Jesus decides to force her to speak. He obliges her to give testimony of her healing - for her good, of course, and for the good of the onlookers and not because he wants the glory. There is help for ourselves and for others in declaring the goodness of God in the storms of our lives whatever form they take, so let's not forgo it.

You cannot imprison the word of the Lord (Luke 9:1-9)
Long ago when I was living in France, I had a sleepless night - it was probably some worry about finding extra helpers for our work with the homeless in down town Toulouse. So, I put on my headphones and on the radio there was an extraordinary piece of music already in full swing with a large orchestra, choirs both jazz and classical, a marching band, children singing and playing kazoos, a rock band and solo speakers and singers. After a few minutes, I realised this was Leonard Bernstein's 'Mass' that I had heard so much about. It's an unbelievable piece and I can't remember ever being so moved and inspired to continue in my work by a piece of music. Well, there's 'Jah Work' by Ben Harper, too: 'You must do the heavy work; so many shall do none. You have got to stand firm; so many shall run.'

In the course of Bernstein's 'Mass' there's a section that declares with power, 'You cannot imprison the Word of the Lord'. 'Come, you great men of power' and consider that Word, is the challenge that Bernstein issues. This section of 'Mass' gives examples from the civil rights movement and anti-war protests, so it's very much of its time, the time of the assassinations of JFK and Bobby Kennedy, Martin Luther King and Malcolm X - it was written for the opening of the Kennedy Centre in New York.

These men were all deeply flawed but what human being, Christian or non-Christian is not weak, and what wouldn't we give in the uncertain and desperate times in which we live to have any one of those four still with us today in their zealous youth and vigour? 'Mass' is a work full of contradictions, doubt and seeming defeat but I don't think it's a coincidence that in recent years the work has had a big comeback in recordings and high-profile performances because there has never been a time in my life and ministry when we've had more need or more hunger for the Word of the Lord. One of my friends showed me a graph with an accompanying newspaper article that proved that, in fact, things are getting better in the world and fewer people are dying. That caught me up short until I realised that it's the type of attacks that are taking place and their graphic reporting that is uniquely distressing now.

This passage could easily have been included in the Bernstein's 'Mass': 'Herod the tetrarch heard about all that was going on. And he was perplexed because some were saying that John had been raised from the dead, others that Elijah had appeared, and still others that one of the prophets of long ago had come back to life. But

Herod said, "I beheaded John. Who, then, is this I hear such things about?" And he tried to see Jesus.'

The 'Great man of power' here is the tetrarch Herod whose namesake had tried to extinguish the Messiah at the beginning of the gospel story by killing all boy babies in the massacre of the innocents. His successor in name somehow thought he had achieved his aim of reducing God to silence by beheading John the Baptist but the Word of the Lord is present in even greater power in Jesus. For Herod, Jesus is like John the Lone Voice raised from the dead or like Elijah returning to call people back to God and to speak truth to power as once the prophet did to Ahab and Jezebel. He thinks of the Old Testament messengers calling people back to the just and loving Law of God. Not only so, but there's not just Jesus doing it but twelve others preaching with power and soon not just twelve but seventy, just as Moses had spread his work of judging the people with seventy elders. 'The Lord gave the word. Great was the company of the preachers.'

This mission is marked by mobility enabled by lightness of means. It results in healing action and deliverance from dark powers. There is restoration and renewal as the proclamation of the Kingdom of God goes forward. We see so much in the world around us of what happens in the world when 'proud hearts and stubborn wills' are in charge but any glimpse we have of the Kingdom of God shows how things are when God is in control.

This passage is about the multiplication of the ministry of Jesus and the impotence of those who would stamp it out. In our day, it is possible to behead individuals who go to the Middle East with a humanitarian aim like James Foley, Peter Kassig and David Haines but the Word of the Lord in mercy, peace and charity cannot be beheaded. Two British nurses come back from West Africa having contracted the Ebola virus but still others go and even one of the two returns for a further period of service. An image after the 'Charlie Hebdo' massacre in Paris showed that if you break a satirical cartoonist's pencil in two, you just end up with two pencils and if you foolishly break those, there are now four. Long ago, Tertullian said, 'The blood of the martyrs is the seed of the Church', while the book of Revelation portrays those who have died for their faith as still alive before God and still calling to him for justice on earth.

There's a song by Labi Siffre we perform with our community choir that even though we never do it justice, we keep on returning to because it has something of this passage about it. It's only a song but it's a powerful one. Surely, the 'something inside so strong' it sings about is the Word of the Lord. 'You cannot imprison the Word of the Lord.'

Do the math (Luke 9 and 10)

In the West there are numerous impressive buildings where people gather for worship while in the streets, men and women can often be seen going about their daily business in clerical garments. For two thousand years society here and by extension all over the world has been affected by Christian teaching on health, education and issues of social justice. Yes, in spite of its decline in many places, the Church is such a well-established institution that it's easy to take it for granted. If you look for the origins of the Church in the gospels, though, it's not easy to find very much at all. There are the few things Jesus says in Matthew's gospel: 'I will build my Church and the gates of hell shall not prevail against it.' There's the linked teaching of Jesus on the role of the apostle Peter as keeper of the keys of the kingdom. It's not a huge amount of explicit material to go on.

As for the origins of Christian ministry, it's a battleground of scholarly argument. In the Book of Acts and the New Testament letters there is some teaching on deacons, pastors, elders and overseers and some description of the establishing of leadership in various places. It's hard to harmonise everything we are told, though, and my own view is that there was considerable variety of forms of leadership in the early days of the church and that it is not really possible to identify any one pattern from that world and impose it on our own. I think we can be flexible about how leadership is exercised and especially about the names we give it in our Christian communities.

Before a huge amount of information comes to us from around the beginning of the second century of the Christian era we learn bits and pieces about the very earliest church from general history and archaeology. Christian meetings seem to have been based on synagogue services - gatherings for worship, teaching and prayer - while these events usually took place in people's homes which were sometimes enlarged to accommodate more attenders.

Maybe we need to be prepared to use a bit of lateral thinking. I think the whole passage in Luke's gospel about the sending on mission first of the twelve, then of the seventy-two with the feeding of the five thousand sandwiched between is about the foundation of the Church. Luke doesn't make a big deal about it: there is no stone-laying ceremony or cutting of a ribbon but there is something important to be discerned all the same.

First of all, Jesus multiples his ministry by twelve, just as God multiplied his promise to Abraham by twelve by extending it to the sons of Jacob and Joseph: so far, so obvious. It is a commonplace to see the dozen disciples as the Fathers of the new Israel as the apostles' eagerness to replace the fallen traitor Judas makes clear. By the way, we are in a world here where the question of the place of women in the community let alone in leadership doesn't seem to occur to anyone. That would never fly today in the West.

The next scene is the miraculous sharing of the bread and fish with the crowd of five thousand coming to hear Jesus and following him around. Jesus gives his followers the responsibility for giving them something to eat and the disciples are embarrassingly aware that they have no resources to do that, having given away their staff, bag, bread, money and extra coat in order to travel light in their mission. Nonetheless, at the suggestion of Jesus, the disciples take what they can muster and it proves to be more than enough. The link with the transmission of spiritual nourishment is fairly easy to make from this incident and many hymns, particularly communion hymns, underline that connection.

What has really caught my attention is the tiny detail of Jesus telling the disciples to get people to sit in groups of fifty to be fed. The size of gatherings is surprisingly interesting and quite a lot of work has been done on it even in secular contexts. In the New Testament there is the little unit of three around Jesus composed of Peter, James and John. Twelve is the number of the disciples and after that, fifty, then 120. As far as I am concerned, fifty is the ideal size for a congregation: everybody gets a chance to know everyone else; each member has a chance to minister, to distribute the bread and the fish but still the group feels fairly large and the pooled resources of such a gathering can achieve much. In church terms, it seems to me that everyone needs two or three intimate supporters, a house group of a dozen may be next, then a congregation of fifty or so before the celebration gathering of 120.

I think that's what we're seeing here in the feeding of the five thousand, and a little basic and playful maths can help. There are five thousand in the crowd (men, incidentally - once again this is a world where women are excluded from the picture). So, there are a hundred groups of fifty - too many for twelve disciples. Moses had the same problem when he was leading the people of Israel through the wilderness on the way from Egypt to Canaan: he couldn't do all the tasks of leadership by himself. So, through his foreign father-in-law, God told Moses to choose seventy people to help him in the work and help provide structure to the wandering nation.

Just a chapter further on in Luke from the sending out of the twelve on mission and the feeding of the five thousand, Jesus sends out seventy-two further disciples on a similar mission. Some early scribes who copied the gospel saw the link with Moses and apparently couldn't resist the temptation to make the connection clear by changing the number to seventy. This time, though, those who are sent are to go on travelling until they find a place that gives them a welcome and then settle down. Then, they are to return to base and report back on how things have been. It seems to me that the local pastoral ministry is right there, as is the regional gathering. With seventy-two groups of fifty, you can take care of the needs of about three and a half thousand people - the number of new Christians on the day of Pentecost, more or less.

Maybe the origins of the Church in the gospels are not so obscure after all.

A woman's place is in the kitchen (Luke 10:38-42)

This story about Martha and Mary always gets people hot under the collar. In the context of Jesus multiplying his ministry by sending out first the twelve then the seventy-two disciples, there's a domestic scene showing two sisters contrasted very strongly indeed. In my opinion, it's never been better portrayed than in the painting 'Christ in the house of Martha and Mary' by Velasquez.

The foreground of this painting shows an old lady scolding a young woman who is obviously overwhelmed with mundane and time-consuming tasks in the kitchen. This is Martha and she has recently been crying as she grinds the garlic and chillies with a pestle and mortar before she starts gutting those bright-eyed fish. Her clothes are dowdy and she appears to be wearing a skirt made out sackcloth but maybe it's an apron. The artist has succeeded brilliantly in capturing her pout and her general air of discontent.

I wonder if that is a serving hatch or a mirror behind Martha, and I'm not sure whether that is that the same old lady standing behind the seated figure. In any case, it's a very different image: here,

Jesus is teaching and a young woman is sitting rapt and relaxed at his feet. She wears flowing drapery in the fashionable colours; she is doe-eyed and her blond tresses tumble to her shoulders. She has just arrived refreshed from the worship group rehearsal where she has been waving a ribbon with demure excitement, lost in wonder, love and praise. This is Mary.

Martha petulantly cries out to Jesus, 'Don't you care that my sister has left me to do all the work?' Jesus replies, 'Martha, Martha, you are worried and upset about many things but Mary has chosen the better place.' Jesus was lucky not to get those eggs broken over his head and the garlic and chilli paste rubbed in.

People always react strongly to this story because everybody knows there are never enough Marthas in the church - somehow you can always get new volunteers for the upfront and glamorous public roles while the cleaning rota has the same few names for years on end. The vigorous twenty-five year old man holds a guitar on the platform while a fragile seventy-five year old woman wields the dustpan and brush after the meeting. But in the setting of the multiplication of ministry, Jesus is making an important point. There are twelve men around him and then seventy-two men who are sent out to establish the Church . . . and then there is Mary.

Luke is known as the gospel for women but I wish he'd gone further still by including yet more of them and reflecting in more depth on their role. Nonetheless, in the historical context he is importantly showing us that women too can be disciples of Jesus. Women, too, can listen at the feet of the Lord, and if they can listen, then presumably they can pass on what they have learned and teach it to others. This type of thinking is important to Luke: we remember the start of the gospel with another Mary giving out the themes to be developed in the course of the book as the mother of Jesus sings the Magnificent. Later on, we will see women as the first witnesses of the risen Christ running to tell the sceptical men about a revolution on earth and in the heavenly places.

Maybe Mary's sister Martha was distracted by the devil and she should have been listening not cooking. I have a lot of respect for the Anglican leader John Stott as a writer but it seems to me he could be wrong about things just as the rest of us can. In Acts chapter 6, the apostles were distracted from their work of teaching and praying by the demands of the Greek women in the early church, some of whom were complaining that they were being missed out of the distribution of common food. The apostles said that it wasn't right for them to be diverted from their main task by these mundane tasks so they appointed seven others to do it. In his 'Bible Speaks Today' commentary on Acts, Stott suggests that by their actions, the apostles successfully avoided what he calls a 'satanic distraction'. Boy, that escalated fast.

I don't think it's a distraction at all to be busy about practical help towards others. I say that even though I am well aware that Jesus rebuked Martha while praising Mary. It's always important to look at the context of a Bible passage by reading what comes before it and what comes after.

By praising Mary, Jesus shows that women can learn at his feet in the same way that the twelve and the seventy-two did. Immediately before the Martha and Mary story we have a tale with many lessons - the parable of the Good Samaritan. I'll have a lot to say about that in my next section but for the moment I'll just mention one thing:

In the parable, two religious teachers go by and they are desperately interested in doing God's work: the priest has important tasks to perform in the temple and he can't afford to get his hands dirty. After all, he is an expert in how to please God and he can't risk ritual contamination from a man who is wounded and who may well be dead. Neither can the Levite who is next on the scene. They both pass by on the other side of the road to avoid getting involved. Jesus commends the third man who stops and binds up the wounds of the victim, taking him to safety, making sure he is cared for and promising to return to check that he is on the road to recovery. Jesus applauds him even though, as a Samaritan, he was about as far outside God's mainstream as it was possible to be according to the definitions and perceptions of the time.

I read the broad context this way: Jesus is multiplying his ministry and he does it by teaching and sending first twelve disciples on mission and then seventy-two. In the midst of all this, a woman, Mary, has a privileged place at the feet of the Master and Jesus emphasises that she is included as a follower of his. The ministry that needs to be multiplied is not just a teaching one, though, nor the kind of things that priests and levites did in the Jerusalem temple. It is practical help, too. The daily tasks and works of mercy are very far from being a 'satanic distraction'.

When you tell others about Jesus, you do God's work; when you get your hands dirty to help others, you do God's work. What's more, in God's Kingdom Mathematics, this is not a case of 50-50 - either or, it is 100-100 - both and.

All the same, I wish Jesus could have spared a kinder word for Martha. I suppose he was making a point about the immediacy of his presence. After all, as he said in another recent context, we will always be surrounded by the poor and always have the opportunity to help in a practical way but the physical presence of Jesus is a precious and limited reality. You can always help others but to sit at the feet of Jesus is rare indeed.

Killer on the road (Luke 10:25-37)

The parable of the good Samaritan is right up there with Adam and Eve, Noah's Ark and the road to Damascus as one of the most famous parts of the Bible and one of the best-loved stories in the world. It's a simple tale and can be quickly told. A man is on a journey but gets robbed and has to lie injured while two religious officials pass by. Eventually, a Samaritan - a despised outsider - stops and helps him. 'Go and do likewise' is the punch-line.

As for the meaning of the story, it's a bit of a test case for how you set about interpreting the Bible as a whole. We were discussing this parable in a church house-group the other day and I pointed out that very often in the past people agreed that you had to look for a deeper meaning under the surface of the text.

Back in the second century of the Christian era, a Bible teacher called Origen said that the man who was mugged represents Adam or humankind as a whole. Jerusalem stands for paradise, and Jericho for the world through which we make our pilgrimage. The robbers represent spiritual enemies while the priest is the law of Moses and the Levite the prophets - both of these parts of the Bible are useful but of limited value in a crisis like the one that has shut us out of God's presence. The good Samaritan himself is Jesus while the inn is the Church. The Samaritan promises to return just as Christ did when he ascended to the Father.

There is much more in this vein in what Origen wrote, but those are the broad outlines. I usually make fun of that type of interpretation as absurdly far-fetched but when I see the names and stature of the many ancient Christian leaders who thought in just this way, I'm forced to reconsider. After all, Chrysostom, Ambrose, Augustine and the rest were not fools and they lived much closer to the time of Jesus than I do. It may be that when Jesus told the story he had that mind-set too and expected people to explore the tale in that kind of way as a matter of course. I'm a lot less dismissive of that type of approach now than I used to be. As LP Hartley put it, 'The past is a foreign country: they do things differently there.'

More recently, another way of interpreting this passage has come to the fore. Mrs Thatcher was the British Prime Minister from 1979 to 1990 and on one famous occasion she used the good Samaritan as an example of compassionate capitalism, saying that people need to have financial resources to helps others: 'No one would remember the Good Samaritan if he had only good intentions; he had money as well.'

The American civil rights leader Martin Luther King also made practical and economic points in the last speech he gave before being assassinated in 1968, 'I've been to the mountaintop.' Anyone who has never seen that speech should stop reading this and look at what he had to say straight away. Go on, do it now - it's easily available on the internet.

I've had to resist the temptation to include a few thousand words of Dr King's speech here but even in a short extract, a powerful interpretation of the parable of the good Samaritan emerges. 'The first question that the priest asked - the first question that the Levite asked was, "If I stop to help this man, what will happen to me?" But then the Good Samaritan came by. And he reversed the question: "If I do not stop to help this man, what will happen to him"' But the civil rights leader goes quite a long way into practicalities and even though what he says is as far as I can judge valid, I do wonder if it comes from the Bible text or whether it has been imposed on it. I'm not saying that we don't need to get rid of modern injustices, like refugee camps, world hunger and food banks for working people in the prosperous West - I'm just trying to get to the meaning of this parable.

When I was training for the Baptist ministry, to read back your own concerns, however valid, into the Bible rather than letting it speak for itself was by far the worst thing you could do when preaching. Instead, we were taught to read and study to try to find out what the original writer and readers of the words of Jesus would have understood by a passage.

In keeping with this principle, we need to see once again that the context of the parable of the good Samaritan is important. The immediate setting is the story about Mary and Martha and the slightly broader situation is the multiplication of the ministry of Jesus. Maybe we need to realise that Christian service is not just about teaching but about helping others, too. 'Go and do likewise' is enough to put paid to the idea that you can spend all of your time sitting at the feet of Jesus because sooner or later he will tell you to go and put his words of love into practice.

There is an even broader context to take into account: the gospel of Luke as a whole and even the whole Bible. Most languages are able to make a particular word stand out of a sentence even though they tend to do so in different ways. In modern English, we have bold type, underlining and italics as well as tone of voice. Here, there is one word that yells and bellows off the page. In New Testament Greek it wouldn't often be the first word in a sentence and so, when it does come first, it has huge emphasis. The word is Samaritan. 'Samaritan he was'.

It's very hard for us to grasp how loaded that word was in the world of the gospels. The Samaritans came from the northern kingdom of Israel which had been conquered long before the region down south around Jerusalem fell to invaders. The original inhabitants had been scattered and the area had been resettled with all kinds of outsider people who had adopted bits and pieces of religious observance that the southerners hated and despised. I have to tread carefully here. I have no problem with immigration at all - in fact, my children are immigrants to the UK because they were born when I was living in France but there are some other groups of people I fear. Perhaps you should have no problem filling out the meaning of the word 'Samaritan' for yourself. 'A supporter of ISIS' might possibly do it for me. For someone else, it might be a transgender person, I suppose.

My interpretation of the parable of the Good Samaritan goes something like this:

The most surprising people in the world can do God's work if it is good work well done. God's law of love was fulfilled not by the Priest and the Levite who were ritually pure but spiritually lacking. We must not be surprised if God blesses us from an unexpected direction because the Kingdom of God is always broader than we think. In the wide context of this part of Luke's gospel, practical ministry is not just for the twelve or the seventy-two or Mary and Martha but for all kinds of people. As for the good news of the gospel message taught by the Bible as a whole, it is for everyone - men, women, children, British and Polish people, Africans and Asians, gay and straight, rich and poor, refugees and free people.

Oh, and, of course, I almost forgot. The Samaritan helped his natural enemy; go and do likewise.

Big Mac at every meal (Luke 11:1-13)

In the Judaism of the time of Jesus, there was a disciplined culture of prayer three times a day which was based on praise, thanksgiving and reverence. There was the 'Shema' - 'hear, O Israel', the 'Kaddish' - 'may his great name be blessed for ever' - and various blessings. This way of life based on prayer was very God-centred and sought to recognise God's greatness and to bow to his will and yet falling into routine was an obvious danger.

The disciples would have been familiar with the system and would have also known about the patterns of the synagogue and the variety of examples in the Psalms with regard to prayer. They would also probably have been aware of some of the dangers of prayer that Jesus warns about - notably, the insincerity which may be built into repetition. All the same, in spite of their prior knowledge and practice, the disciples were struck by the example of both John the Baptist and Jesus in prayer. They must have seen and have been impressed by something different in John and Jesus for them to be sufficiently moved for them to ask to be taught how to pray as these masters did.

Probably the most important thing a Christian leader can do is to teach how to pray and show how to do it, so what a privilege it is to be able to eavesdrop on what Jesus said when he gladly replied to the disciples' request. He doesn't fob them off by saying 'I don't know, I just do it.' He doesn't tell them it's too personal to be spoken of.

I intend to look at all of what Jesus says about prayer in this part of Luke in one go and then focus on the Lord's Prayer as given in this gospel but I think what he says can be summed up in one word. Prayer is relationship: yes, God is other but he is not remote. If I wanted to sum up prayer as relationship in one word, it would be, 'Father'. The Lord's Prayer is so familiar to us that the impact of that one word is easily missed but the whole of the teaching Jesus gives in Luke builds on that one, practically universal word. I say 'practically' because I know that not everyone is fortunate enough to be able to have a positive reaction to the word 'father'. Nonetheless, even these excluded people can experience the welcome of Father.

There are three parts to Jesus's teaching and they are given in parables. As usual, the parable rule applies. In case you don't know about the parable rule, it is that there is only one point to a parable. Parables are not allegories where every detail of a story has a parallel, but stories with just one meaning. Look at my section on the Good Samaritan for an example of the arbitrary nature of the alternative, allegorical view.

In the first story we are meant to imagine ourselves in a situation of need with only one friend who can help. Even though it is the middle of the night, we decide we really have no option but to go to that friend for help all the same. Surprisingly, though, the key word in this first story about the midnight knocking at the door is not a word about relationship or friendship at all but, instead, we are meant to focus on 'boldness'. We are to go to God with boldness. Yes, we do have a relationship with the father but it is our boldness that will win the day.

The next tale is one of the rare ones where knowledge of New Testament Greek is useful rather than just a trump card to be pulled out and thumped on the table when the argument is not going well. This time, I want us to imagine a situation which could surely never arise outside the strange world of the Christian minister: you go to visit someone and it doesn't really matter whether you see them or not. Actually, you hope they are not in because that will save you the bother of talking to them. Here, on the other hand, is a situation where you know your friend is there and you're jolly well going to keep on knocking until they answer. Here the key word is 'persistence' - you go on asking, seeking and knocking, as the New Testament Greek tells you to do.

The third tale is to do with common sense and its lesson is so obvious that it almost feels insulting to spell it out. We are meant to realise that it's clear that someone who wishes you well and can help you is going to help you. This is so obvious but Jesus thought it was worth saying and teaching in terms of a father who gives only good things to a child.

There are one or two things to point out, of course. For

instance, as parents, we don't always give our children what they ask for just because they ask. That would often be very irresponsible and they would probably end up with every meal a Big Mac and large fries with a plastic toy. What we need to imagine, though, is some situation where you're asking God for help and you already know that he is your Father. Now, you need to realise that whatever happens, he is not going to respond to your request with something that will harm you. He's going to give you what you need under the circumstances - circumstances of which, quite often, you are only partly aware.

So, before we go on to the Lord's Prayer, we learn from these three parables of Jesus that prayer is not a formal activity directed towards an impersonal God who can't connect with us but is communication with our Father. This Father is moved by boldness and he values persistence on the part of those outside the door, knocking. What's more, he knows what is best for his children. This is a solid foundation for what comes next in the Lord's Prayer itself.

Father (Luke 11:1-4)
There's some debate about whether the Lord's Prayer is a set form of words that we should employ as it stands or a template we should use when praying. In the part of the Church where I have ministered, we set great store by what we call extemporary prayer and we've been sceptical about written prayers - although, to be honest, that seems to

be changing recently. All the same, even in quite high-pressure situations, such is my allegiance to the principle of spontaneous prayer that I've practically never written a prayer to be read later and I passed up the chance to write a prayer for a book even though it would have been very good for my career, such as it is, to do so. I well remember praying at a large rally in the South of France attended by thousands and I was so nervous that I forgot to take my sunglasses off - something that earned me a lot of teasing - but I still prayed spontaneously. I understand the arguments in the other direction - the Holy Spirit inspires writing as well as speaking; he leads thinking, formulation, framing and expression all along the line. All the same, I feel part of a tradition of prayer that wants to emphasise the heart of the person praying in the moment.

The Lord's Prayer seems different, though: it is a formulation that, on the whole, people of all traditions are happy to use as it stands. Many of us can testify that, in the extremity of suffering, when all other language is lost, this prayer retains its power and an 'Amen' to this form of words may well be the last word spoken aloud by a person returning home to God. In the congregation, maybe the Lord's Prayer is spoken to close a meeting, or to bring other prayers together into a common utterance. Perhaps, it is used to teach about prayer. In my last church, we used it every Sunday after the offering in order to express the fact that we wanted to put our money into the Kingdom of

God and its progress. We used it because we wanted to bring a symbol of our very selves with the offering and place that at the service of the kingdom of God. So, we brought ourselves and our possessions to him near the beginning of every service and used the Lord's Prayer to do this.

My mind takes me back to Thomas Hardcastle, an early Baptist pastor in Bristol in the seventeenth century. He was ejected from the Church of England in 1662 and was imprisoned numerous times for his illegal preaching before dying young. In prison in Bristol, Hardcastle wrote letters to the church which went on meeting in secret in his absence and in the Broadmead Baptist Church records those precious epistles are bound together with some sermons and some teaching to the children including a series on the Apostles' Creed and one on the Lord's Prayer. Now, I don't think anyone would seriously doubt Hardcastle's commitment to standing for the principles I love, although, as a former vicar in the established Church his understanding of forms of prayer may well have differed from my own. So, I respect Hardcastle when he sees the Lord's Prayer as a model to be taught to the children.

The Lord's Prayer as recorded by Luke is quite a bit shorter than what we recite nowadays. Either Matthew expanded on the original material whatever form it took or Luke took Matthew's version and pruned it. Using a little elementary scholarship and looking at the alternative readings, I think that what we have in Luke is probably the closest we're going to get to what Jesus taught and that Matthew amplified what he found.

Jesus says that in prayer we address Father. Not, 'Our Father' or 'Our Father which art in heaven', but Father. Once again, I could probably stop there but Jesus tells us to go on to pray for God's name to be sanctified. I take this to mean that we should pray for God to be taken into account in a world that often ignores him. An alternative reading asks that the Holy Spirit should come upon us and make us clean but this suggestion seems to me to be later and to take away from the main focus of this part of the prayer: God and his kingdom in the visible world. This is a huge agenda to do with longing for justice and mercy in all we see. I remember once that a church member in France criticised me for mentioning the politicians of the day by name in prayer but I just went right on doing it because as we pray we should be wrestling with the way things actually are in the world in which we live. After all, because of Bible prophecy we have a vision of how things could be and how far we fall short.

I'm keeping the rest of what I say about the Lord's Prayer very brief - because what we have in Luke is a series of short sayings. They remind me of the *Pensées* of the French mathematician and philosopher Blaise Pascal, because they are short utterances suggesting a lifetime of reflection and refinement.

Pascal said, 'All of humanity's problems arise from being unable to sit in a room alone' and 'To make light of philosophy is to be a true philosopher'. For his part, Jesus said, 'Give us our daily bread', and in that short saying, all of our needs are expressed in five words along with all the sources of conflict in the world as people fight for sustenance and for the land where crops can be planted.

'Forgive us our sins,' says Jesus, reminding us that if we hope to be forgiven by God we should be prepared to forgive others.

Jesus goes on, 'Don't lead us into evil,' and I remember that I am often happily and easily led in the wrong direction. This is such a problem for me and for everyone I know that I wonder if a conversion of my will is ever going to be possible at all.

That's it for the Lord's Prayer in Luke. The way we end in public worship goes, 'For thine is the kingdom, the power and the glory for ever and ever' but this conclusion comes from Matthew's gospel and, anyway, it appears to be an extract from a prayer of King David grafted on to what Jesus said to provide a suitable close. When you look at it like that, the Lord's Prayer in Luke's gospel doesn't amount to much but in reality it is enough and to spare. The main word is 'Father' and that one word is really sufficient in itself. The three pictures of prayer from the parables of Jesus really sum up how it is between us and our Father: we are to relate to him with boldness, persistence and on the basis of the recognition that he knows best.

That last element is probably the hardest for us to accept, because it implies weakness and submission on our part and that doesn't come easily to us at all no matter how needy and lost we may be.

Christian Mindfulness (Luke 12:13-48)
We hear a lot about Mindfulness these days - it's a buzz word in the media, there are courses on it and it even features in school life in some places. Mindfulness has three manifestations that need to be differentiated. It originates as a spiritual practice in Buddhism and is used seriously in psychology but it is in self-help movements that most of us are likely to come across it. One definition of mindfulness is a 'moment to moment awareness of present events' and it includes being attentive to our emotions, thoughts and sensations.

It seems to me that the second and third types of mindfulness don't pose much of a problem for Christians. For instance, in psychology, it is used under expert supervision to help people distance themselves from the press of modern life and assess things objectively in order to reduce stress and anxiety. In self-help fads it can be easily caricatured as 'McMindfulness' and it can easily become just another commodity in the supermarket of ideas that ironically increases an unhelpful absorption on the self and its preoccupations. As for the Buddhist type of mindfulness, it is problematic for the Christian not in itself but because of the cosmological baggage behind it. Unlike

Buddhism with its belief in reincarnation, Christianity teaches a linear history of the universe and the world and a linear destiny for each of us, too. As the Bible puts it, we live and die once and then comes the judgement.

While we may be cautious about buying into the current fashion, we should be proud of the fact that in Jesus we have the greatest master of mindfulness of them all. The conclusion of the Sermon on the Mount has clear teaching on this but so does Luke chapter twelve. In a systematic way, Jesus tells us first what we should avoid setting our minds on and then gives us advice on what should preoccupy us instead.

Like the incomparale teacher he is, Jesus begins with a story that sums up all of his teaching. Told in a context of a family dispute about an inheritance, this parable about a rich fool who tore down his barns to build bigger ones but who died before they could be used teaches us important lessons even before Jesus goes into detail about mindfulness. It tells us we should be content with what we have or, rather, to be content with having what we need today rather than wasting our lives in wondering whether we can get still more in the future. To be wrapped up in oneself is to be wrapped up in something that is literally ephemeral - of the day. We learn from what Jesus says that there is another way to be rich than by having a lot of possessions - we can be rich towards God.

The idea of having treasures in heaven is developed by Jesus in the positive part of what he has to say. It's to do with serving others and I'll be looking at that in my next section but in this one I want to look in more detail at what Jesus tells us is unworthy of our attention.

Jesus gives us two real challenges in telling us not to set our hearts on what we eat or on what we wear. Of course, we all need to eat something and to have some clothes to put on but I have done a bit of playful research on this. Instead of going into a charity shop for garments and stocking the kitchen cupboard from a discount supermarket it is possible to make a big statement about the level of your prosperity by going out for the most expensive meal in Great Britain at £1500 a head. For that price you get a variety of dishes, including sea slugs, cod stomachs and even swallow's nest stew. As for clothes, I've heard that the price of a handbag is often a mark of one's status, so I looked on the internet, thinking at first that the most expensive one might be as much as £100. I was hopelessly naive with every guess I made because I found one at over a quarter of a million pounds. It's quite a long way from the apostle Paul saying that he was just happy with enough to eat and something to wear and that he had known plenty and want and had learned to be content with either. As for John the Baptist, he wore camel hair and ate locusts and wild honey.

Jesus finishes this section by giving us some advice that we hear as overwhelmingly negative. First of all, we need to realise that as a 'little flock' we don't have access to the levers of power here on earth. It may well be the Father's will to give us the kingdom but it turns out to be an unenviable legacy because it is a kingdom of weakness, poverty and vulnerability. Not only so, but we are to sell what we have and give the proceeds to the poor to attain it.

Now, we need to start where we are and I'm conscious that not many people reading this are likely put this teaching of Jesus into practice in a literal sense. Most of us have never seen anyone do it and we are used to explaining it away. After all, if we gave everything away we should become poor ourselves and others would have to step in to help us. Some commentators feel that this is exactly where the Jerusalem church in the Acts of the Apostles came unstuck - they gave everything away and others had to organise a collection to come to their aid.

Maybe the way we should start to take seriously what Jesus says is to try to be careful not to set our hearts on what we eat and what we wear and I reckon that to cultivate a simpler, more modest lifestyle is a beginning worth considering. I feel a nagging uncertainty, though. I think of some who have taken Jesus at his word -people like Saint Francis, the Catholic activist Dorothy Day and the missionary to Africa C.T. Studd. Above all, I remember that Jesus was not content just to teach us about the simplicity of total reliance on God: he demonstrated it. He told us himself that animals and birds had their homes but that he had none. And this he did for us. As the apostle Paul puts it, 'Though he was rich, for your sake he became poor so that through his poverty you might become rich.' The early childhood of Jesus was that of a hunted refugee while his adult life was that of a misunderstood wandering teacher who was betrayed to his powerful critics by a friend and abandoned to his fate by his closest followers. His death was that of a naked criminal denied even a modicum of justice and mercy.

Yet it is the good pleasure of the Father to give Jesus the Kingdom and to have him seated at his own right hand. The kind of mindfulness we should have is not to do with possessions at all. Paul says, 'Have this mind among you that was in Christ Jesus who, being in very nature God, did not consider equality with God something to be used to his own advantage; rather, he made himself nothing by taking the very nature of a servant being made in human likeness. And being found in appearance as a man, he humbled himself by becoming obedient to death even death on a cross!'

My very good friend the vacuum cleaner - positive mindfulness (Luke 12:35-48)

In June 2016 British people voted in a referendum to decide whether the United Kingdom should stay in the European Union or begin the long process of leaving it. It was a very divisive campaign during which those who wanted to remain focused on the economic uncertainties of a future outside Europe while those who wanted to lead us towards the exit spoke interminably about the dangers supposedly linked with immigration. On the day that a Member of Parliament was murdered in the streets of her own constituency, a poster appeared on billboards showing a line of refugees and with captions designed to whip up fear of the stranger. It was uncomfortably reminiscent of one particular, identifiable Nazi propaganda photograph.

No campaign should be exclusively negative and after he tells us what we should refuse to set our hearts on, Jesus points out what is worthy of our attention instead. The context is one of a future judgement that is absolutely inevitable but which God appears to be delaying for the moment, creating for us an invaluable space in which we can work for the good. In the crisis of future judgement, some will suffer ruin, according to the Lord, but this reality is not meant to make us despair but to urge us on to be more positively mindful in the way we live.

Once again there's a vivid word picture involved and this time it is the image of a large household that needs to be run efficiently while the master is away. We are all familiar with the idea that some are managers and some are workers in this type of set-up. This seems to be a comforting idea for British people because in successive generations, hugely successful television series have portrayed it - 'Upstairs and Downstairs' and 'Downton Abbey' are a couple of the programmes I have in mind.

However, in a twist familiar to all students of the teaching of Jesus, the household in which we find ourselves while we await his return is not like that. Here, the servants are to serve each other and the manager is to care for the staff and give them their food at the right time. It's a household where everybody is equal and all are expected to serve. So, it's a mutually interdependent community of service.

Unfortunately, people being what they are, while the master is away, the servants begin to take it easy and the manager to lord it over those he is supposed to cherish. In the context, this is clearly a picture of the Christian Church of all ages waiting for Jesus to return. Maybe the manager is the pastor of the Christian community – and, certainly, it's no way to take care of the household of God to exploit people and give yourself airs. Strangely enough, though, Jesus doesn't make that connection explicit even when Peter presses him on it - instead, he leaves it open: 'Who is the faithful and wise manager the master puts in charge?'

It's a great question. In the churches I know - mainly Baptist communities - we are not supposed to have a hierarchy and each member plays many roles. At different times, one person might be a cook, an accountant, a cleaner or a teacher. Many people have a spell as a youth worker, as a member of the leadership team or spend time and energy helping out in the many different departments that make up a thriving fellowship. Once, I worked with a team of young people on short term mission who complained about being given what they called 'menial tasks' to do, like delivering leaflets. I had to point out that even though I had the title of Reverend and four degrees including a doctorate, I still had to deliver leaflets and I was happy to do it. The repetitive nature of the job pleases me somehow.

So, I think in answer to the question of Jesus about the identity of the faithful and wise manager, I'd say, 'If the cap fits, wear it.' The way I see it, the positive mindfulness Jesus is talking about as we await his return goes something like this:

There is only one real master and that is the head of the Christian Church - Jesus himself. One day, he will judge our work but for the moment we are all his valued servants during our time on earth and we should look after one another with loving care. If we find ourselves in a situation where we are leading, the position is not to go to our heads but instead we are to look for situations where we can wash one another's feet with humility just as Jesus did for his disciples. Not only so, we are not to make sure there is a film crew there when we get out the bowl and towels and take to our knees. The kitchen will be familiar to the wise and faithful manager and the vacuum cleaner an old friend. When trouble comes to one of our fellow servants, we will already know where they live, whether the doorbell works or not and whether to use the front or the back door.

The apostles Paul and Peter in their letters also use the picture of a household to describe what we are as the Church but the focus is on the metaphorical building itself rather than on the running of the domestic economy. For both of them, we are God's building site and each of us is a stone in the edifice which has Christ for its cornerstone. Paul also has the image of a human body whose head is Christ but whose every part has value and whose less spectacular members are treated with special dignity.

There is this type of positive mindfulness in the words of a famous song by Graham Kendrick called 'The Servant King': 'So let us learn how to serve and in our lives enthrone him. Each other's needs to prefer, for it is Christ we're serving.'

Why, God, why? (Luke 13:1-9)

Human suffering is a great challenge to faith. There is hope even in the worst of situations, though, because God specialises in taking bad situations and turning them around for his wider purposes.

The Bible is full of people trying to make sense of human tragedy by speculating on factors that are, in fact, unfathomable.

Once, they brought a blind man to Jesus and asked whether it was he who sinned or his parents, that he should have been born like that. Jesus dismisses the question as irrelevant. Another time, God healed a man in Lystra through the ministry of Paul and Barnabas and the crowd jumped to the conclusion that they must be the gods Zeus and Hermes in human form. Incidentally, Barnabas appears to have learned that if you want to be taken for a wise leader, you should hold your peace because the onlookers assumed that he was the strong and silent senior god. It was a roller-coaster ride for Paul later on: when he escaped from a shipwreck people thought he must be a murderer protected by evil forces but when he was bitten by a snake and survived, once again people wanted to worship him. I do hope Paul had a sense of humour. The Old Testament book of Job is a long meditation on the meaning of suffering during which many solutions are debated at great length until the conclusion is reached. It goes like this: we don't know, but God is God anyway.

You would have to be hard-hearted indeed not to spend time daily thinking about these matters in connection with today's world. When we pray for our missionaries in Nepal caught up in an earthquake and they turn out to be safe, we are rightly relieved but we also catch ourselves wondering whether if we'd prayed harder we might have helped to save more people's lives. Maybe God is angry with that country because it is primarily Buddhist. I don't think that, by the way, but it's the type of solution people sometimes come up with.

The problem of suffering is a huge one in philosophy and, to cut to the chase, we simply don't know why people are caught up in it. In the gospels, folk didn't hesitate to bring the newspapers to Jesus and ask him about particular stories, though, and we have a record of the answers he gave to two of these groups of concerned people when they asked about about a military atrocity in Jerusalem and an accident where a tower fell and there were fatalities. Where was God in these events? Did he cause them or simply allow them to happen? Could he have prevented them? If not, why not? If he could have stepped in, why didn't he? Does God exercise judgements before the Day of Judgement?

The two stories are different and they need to be considered separately even though Luke lumps them together. The first is about a protest in the Jerusalem Temple against the Roman governor Pilate, who had the audacity to use money considered holy by the Jews to provide a better water supply for the city. A source outside the Bible tells us that Pilate sent in plain clothes policemen with concealed cudgels to mingle with the crowd but that they overstepped the mark against excitable people in the melee and killed some. We can't know at this distance who to blame, conservative people who don't want money spend on hygiene, a government which is not sensitive to public feeling in planning public works or the brutality of law enforcement officers. Incidentally, this is first century Jerusalem, not inner-city USA or GB.

This first news story doesn't seem too difficult to interpret to me. Given that, as human beings we have, as the sixteenth century Reformer Calvin put it, the image of God in ruins in us, then crowds get out of hand and in the clampdown, people get hurt. In war, innocent men, women and children are killed and forced onto the road by other pawns in a bigger game. Any sin involved in causing these deaths and displacements is not only in violent individuals but in the institutions for which they work. So, we strive to reform not only human nature but also the structures of society itself. Jesus, though, is not so cautious. He brings in the perspective of eternity and judgement even here. He says there is a lesson to be learned by each of us that life is short and that we should be mindful of that in how we live for the remainder of our days as we await the judgement of God.

As far as I am concerned, the second story about the tower that fell, killing the builders, is a whole lot more difficult. Maybe there was an earthquake or maybe the manager was guilty of cutting corners. If the latter, then we should speak out for better building regulations and refuse to exploit workers by putting them in danger for profit. If the former, once again, we simply don't know. In the kind of world we live in there are tsunamis, earthquakes and other unpredictable events. Historically, Jesus seems in his reply to be drawing a lesson for the Jewish people. He knew that Jerusalem would be destroyed just a few decades after his own death and resurrection and he is concerned that his hearers should use their few remaining years to turn back to God. The wider lesson he gives to us all is the same one that he gave in the context of the Temple massacre, namely that life is short and that we should take that into account in a mindful way as we live in the light of God's future judgement.

It surprises me that by offering a moral rather than a meaning, Jesus doesn't address the question of random suffering at all. I wondered if Google could do any better, so I typed in, 'Why earthquakes happen.' I got hundreds of pages of scientific reasoning in return to do with tectonic plates and changing weather patterns as well as what I was really looking for - many reams of what's called 'theodicy' - attempts to justify God's ways. Much of this theodicy was familiar to me. After all, the questions I asked near the beginning of this section are much older than Christianity itself: if God can alleviate suffering, why doesn't he? If he can't, is he God?

The Bible does sometimes show natural disasters as judgements on sin - the opponents of Moses perish in this way as does the whole natural creation at the time of the Ark - but that capricious God is tantalisingly hard to love if perilously easy to fear. In the New Testament, earthquakes are sometimes signs to explain the nature of the world we live in. For instance, according to Matthew's gospel, when Jesus died on the cross, there was a rupture in the created order, the graves of holy people were opened and the saints of the Old Testament were seen alive again. For Paul in his letter to the Romans, God's creation is groaning as if in the pains of childbirth while waiting for the true meaning of history to be revealed. Jesus himself elsewhere says that that famines and earthquakes are signs of the beginning of those birth pains.

I'm not being dismissive or facetious but I can't imagine any of that material would help me very much if I were camping out amidst the ruins of my apartment block with my family missing and all amenities cut off. In the safety of their studies philosophers say that the problem of evil is given some meaning when acts of heroism are done and when people pull together. Many Christians talk, a little too complacently for my liking, about great opportunities to share the gospel when hearts are opened to eternal questions: the catastrophic events in Haiti in 2010 were often interpreted in this way. Of course, when bad things happen to us or those we love, we ask serious questions and we ask them more urgently than I am here and these theoretical answers are nowhere near enough to help with the pain people feel in the instant and then have to live with for life.

Maybe you want to know what I really think. My working model after thirty years in Christian ministry and after some experience of apparently meaningless human suffering is that God brings good out of bad things that are going to happen anyway. I think that the cross and the resurrection show that God in Jesus knows questioning from personal experience but specialises in answering questions with redemption. So, whenever I am asked for help by those who are hurting, I always tell people to be vigilant to see what God might decide to do to 'turn their suffering' as the Psalmist puts it. All the same, I don't think I know very much and I make no claim to being an expert in this field. Sometimes it becomes hallowed ground, that's all, and I hope I know how to be silent when that happens.

In or out? (Luke 13:10-19)
As his ministry to the insiders at the synagogue comes to an end, Jesus continues to make the same gracious invitations to them as he did at the beginning of his work. From now on though, his actions will be directed mainly to those outside the walls of the religious establishment.

When we are reached the end of the campaign culminating in the referendum to decide whether the UK was to stay in the European Union or begin the process of leaving it, leading politicians toured the British Isles to try and convince people to change sides or stop wavering and decide. In the last few days of any campaign, there is no room for improvisation and the message stays the same from place to place.

Every so often in the gospels we notice Jesus giving another version of an old and familiar message and it's with a feeling of déjà vu that we read of Jesus back in the synagogue on a Saturday and carrying out a controversial healing. It recalls the start of his synagogue ministry in Mark's gospel where he causes uproar by making the man with a shrivelled hand whole again. It's hard to believe that Jesus would do the same again given that the first time it led to death threats and murderous plotting but it seems he just can't stop doing good. Not only so, but he expresses himself in exactly the same way as he did before by asking if it is right to do good or evil on the Sabbath. The result is the same, too, with some filled with joy at the works of a merciful God and others humiliated and full of envy and spite.

The reason for this repetition is that Mark tells about the beginning of the ministry of Jesus to the synagogue as an institution while Luke shows it coming to an end. For the last time, Jesus comes to this religious world and gives it one more chance simply because it is in his nature to keep on trying to persuade people. Once, he told a story about a vine that refused to produce any grapes until it was obvious to everyone that it had to be uprooted and burnt - except that Jesus said it should be given just one more year to bear fruit. It is characteristic of Jesus in his dealings with us - stubborn human beings

- to say, 'Who knows, maybe this time?'

So, Jesus bowls them an easy, underarm delivery in the synagogue by making a woman bent over for eighteen years able to stand up straight and tall once again. What's not to like in that? HG Wells said of Beatrice Webb that 'she saw men as specimens walking.' Unfortunately, for those observing Jesus with a spirit of judgement, this woman was just a case, just a statistic: both she and Jesus himself had to be made to slot into a legalistic system where healing on the Sabbath was not permitted no matter how much good was achieved or how much God was glorified.

For Jesus, though, the individual always comes first and the system nowhere - we are not specimens, or cases or statistics to him but people whom he loves and wants to kiss and make whole. It's no coincidence that Jesus describes this lady as a 'daughter of Abraham' because in Luke's gospel he is always trying to reintroduce people into the Judaism of faith and relationship that already existed when Abraham lived, long before the Law of Moses was given. Abraham had no Temple and no list of legalistic observances but instead lived in immediacy and intimacy with the God who wants people back on exactly those terms with such intensity that he is unwilling to wait a moment longer than necessary, even if it is on a Sabbath that he introduced himself. In human terms, it wouldn't have mattered if this woman had had to wait just a few more hours after eighteen years of agony but God is impulsive to bless and Jesus acts on that willingness and hopes that the rulers of religion will catch the contagion of joy. Spoiler alert: they don't. 'One more year and maybe it'll bear fruit', says Jesus of the vine until, one day, it is too late. We see in Luke chapter thirteen the end of the campaign where the votes are finally cast in the synagogue against Jesus. From here it's a short step to the murderous plot that ends at the cross of Calvary.

There is another echo of the beginning of Jesus's earlier synagogue ministry now that the whole thing is coming to an end. He told a story about a grain of mustard seed then and he tells it again now but the funny thing is that he tells the same story to mean two different things - once at the beginning and once more at the end. At the start, he is talking about the smallness of the seed that grows into a huge tree and this version applies to Jesus as he begins his mission as a physically limited, visible man trudging from synagogue to synagogue where he preaches and the listeners can take or leave what he says. Some decide to follow and are delighted to the extent that they want to make him king so much do they love the show. In this early context, the mustard seed parable means that in the apparent insignificance of the ministry of a wandering rabbi is the sowing of the seed of the mighty Kingdom of God.

This later time, Jesus tells the same story for a different reason. Now, not the smallness of the seed but the massive size of the tree that grows from it is in view. If this is the end of the synagogue ministry of Jesus then it is the beginning of something else far greater. If the synagogue doesn't want Christ, then the wider world shall have him.

For me, this is Luke's version of the time in John's gospel when some Greeks come to the disciples wanting to see Jesus and from then on his ministry turns outwards to people of all nations and all backgrounds. There, too, Jesus speaks of a seed falling into the ground and dying so that it can bear much fruit not in the limited setting of the synagogue but in the whole world.

Human exclusions are invented and implemented by human beings and not by God because now that the synagogue ministry is at an end, all kinds of outsider people can be included in the embrace of Jesus. The apostle Paul caught the spirit of the God of inclusion when he wrote that, 'in Christ there is neither Jew nor Gentile, neither slave nor free, nor is there male and female, for you are all one in Christ Jesus.' As for the apostle John, he made the astounding proclamation that 'Christ is the atoning sacrifice for our sins, and not only for ours but also for the sins of the whole world.' Some think John was being a little reckless in expressing himself in this way but maybe we can never exaggerate the extent of God's love and his ability to save. After all, as Paul puts it, 'God was in Christ reconciling the world to himself.'

In keeping with all this, we can say that no basis of human

exclusion we can think of in terms of status, sexuality or skin can prevent anyone from coming to relationship with God in Christ. In the language used by Jesus, innumerable birds of all types can find a perch in the mighty oak, the great baobab or the giant redwood that is the spreading, growing tree of the Kingdom of God.

'Lesser breeds without the law' (Luke 13:22-35)
Now we come to the meaty heart of the gospel of Luke. After he finishes his ministry in the synagogue with an easy invitation to recognise his grace in a wonderful healing, Jesus, having been rejected by the authorities, begins to operate on the fringes between the synagogue and the wider world of the gentiles. In this space he gives teaching that has importance for both and shows that the grace of God is far more inclusive than any religious institution had previously thought.

Jesus is mainly in dialogue with the Pharisees during this part of the gospel and we need to know a bit about them. They get such a bad press in the gospels that it's a relief to see that for once some are on Jesus's side, at least at the beginning.

These Pharisees come to Jesus wanting to help him escape from a common enemy - the same King Herod who had just arranged for the assassination of John the Baptist in prison. It's helpful to remember that in many ways Jesus and the Pharisees were singing from the same hymn sheet because they both wanted to please God but set about it in different ways. They are so close to his own point of view in so many respects that we can only say that Jesus is cruel to be kind just as we often are with those closest to us. It's good to know that his warnings were not entirely in vain and that some Pharisees believed in him during his ministry while others were early converts after the death and resurrection of Jesus: the book of Acts tells us this.

The question of how to please God is a basic one and I suppose that most people in a broadly Christian culture will reach for a list of 'churchy' things like prayer, church attendance and reading the Bible. I've already said a number of times in this book that God likes good things and, to a certain extent, Jesus appears to buy into this notion of pleasing God by our efforts when he uses the language of sticking to the narrow way and being persistent in knocking at the door marked prayer.

But there's a twist. According to Jesus here the people who enjoyed such great opportunities of fellowship with him while he walked this earth are largely shut out in the end. They have eaten and drunk with him and listened to his table teaching as well as his more formal teaching in the synagogues but for all that, they are excluded while the ones who are let in are, as far as the Judaism of the time is concerned, little better than a rabble - people from north south east and west.

From this distance, we tend to see the Pharisees as an undifferentiated mass but there were different types of Pharisee and, once again, I am indebted to William Barclay for his description of different groups in their movement. Barclay is popularising more scholarly sources and some of what he says is humorous - and even the 'Jewish Encyclopedia' describes some of these categories as 'eccentric fools' - but we should never forget that the aim of all of them is the deadly earnest one of being acceptable to God.

So, there were the 'shoulder Pharisees' who displayed their good works for all to see and were closely related to the 'wait-a-little Pharisees' who used to try the patience of others while they carried out their lengthy ritual observances. The 'bleeding Pharisees' considered that a wound received by walking into a wall rather than looking at a woman was a badge of honour while the 'ever-reckoning Pharisees' were forever calculating whether or not their account with God was in credit. The 'fearing Pharisees' would tend to think that they were falling short in God's judgement while the 'hump-backed Pharisees' lived with exaggerated humility, hoping to be acceptable to him in that way.

There are, too, the 'God-loving Pharisees' who consciously imitated Abraham in faith and charity. If the woman in the synagogue who received her healing was described by Jesus as a daughter of Abraham, then this party within the wider grouping of the Pharisees was surely not far from the Kingdom of God, a kingdom in which, according to the Lord, Abraham, Isaac and Jacob are to be found alongside an immigrant throng who somehow manage to find their way in in front of those who expend great efforts to enter but whose exertion goes in the wrong direction.

Here in the Kingdom is a community composed either of people who loved God long before the Law of Moses was given in cloud and majesty and awe or who have never even heard of it because they are beyond the pale.

The question of the correct interpretation of the relationship between the Law of Moses and the Christian faith is a difficult one and libraries of books have been written in attempts to answer it. We remember that in the Sermon on the Mount in Matthew's gospel Jesus says that not a pen stroke will ever be taken away from the Law as far as God is concerned. Unfortunately, even a casual reading of that great discourse shows that the Lord describes the Law in a way that makes it clear that no one could ever even come close to fulfilling what it requires. He applies it not only to actions but also to the secret world of thoughts and attitudes where none of us could ever be said to be wholly innocent of wrong motives.

The apostle Paul again and again comes within an ace of saying the Law of Moses no longer applies to Christians but never actually comes out and states that clearly. Maybe he is at his best when he calls the Law a schoolmaster to bring us to Christ but in any case his most compelling illustrations of faith in his letters to the Romans and Galatians are not about Moses at all but about about Abraham the man of faith before the Law was given. Further on in the New Testament, the letter to the Hebrews describes our own efforts at righteousness as being like filthy rags as far as God is concerned. It seems that the best the Law can ever do is to reveal our need not of more and yet more personal righteousness but of forgiveness and a new start.

It seems that the overwhelming majority of the Pharisees at the time of Jesus failed to grasp that and tried to live under Moses rather than following Abraham. I wonder how many of us today fall into the same trap and will tend to try and plead our case with God rather than live by faith and be content to point to the finished work of Jesus on the cross. This doesn't come easily to us because it goes against our pride and self-reliance and even offends our sense of justice but that's how it must be. In that sense, it's a narrow door and few find it.

Let's get this party started (Luke 13:34 -14:24)
Now that Jesus has begun to operate on the margins between the synagogue and the wider world, the stories about the inclusion of strangers come crowding in. The first is about a narrow door which the Pharisees tried hard to enter but by striving in the wrong way. This

was in spite of their close observation of Jesus and their table fellowship with the one who took pains to explain how to get in. Instead, a rabble from 'the four corners of the imagined world' file through the gateway in an orderly manner.

In the next tale, the picture changes but the teaching remains the same. This time, we are at a wedding feast but first, as so often with Jesus, there is an easy test question to answer - one you would have to struggle to get wrong. For a start, this time Jesus is speaking in a private house rather than in the public setting of the synagogue and, ironically, it is easier to speak your mind at the dinner table than in the pulpit, that place of fearless proclamation where every word is weighed in the balance and judged by the listeners. So eager is Jesus to help the Pharisees to return to God that he helps them out and meets them halfway. He asks the hard and disputed question first about whether it is lawful to heal on the Sabbath or not. Then, after he heals a man comes the easy and consensual question about what you should do if your donkey, your ox or your son falls into a well on a Sabbath. To save or not to save?

The latter is an easy question because the Pharisees had already had this discussion with rival groups and come to the obvious conclusion that it is clearly lawful to do this kind of good work even on the Sabbath. The inference Jesus is making is clear: it is surely far better to heal someone on a holy day than to rescue a beast from a dark, dank place.

Even this reasoning is not enough for the opponents of Jesus to come round to his opinion. It is one thing to have correct beliefs and quite another to follow Christ as one of his disciples. I took a group of young people to an indoor climbing centre the other day and because I'm a little creaky in the joints, afraid of heights and lazy I decided to stay in the viewing gallery. There, I found a pile of magazines about mountaineering, showing the equipment needed to scale the highest peaks in the world and explaining the techniques needed. I returned from that outing as a great expert on climbing - but only in my head. My beliefs were correct but my practice would quickly have revealed that my knowledge was entirely theoretical.

Next comes yet another picture of the Kingdom of God that takes the hospitality of God as its starting point. This time we are at a wedding banquet. The lavish wedding meal is one of the most prominent images in the Bible, speaking as it does of friendship with God and with one another. The Communion meal of the Last Supper is part of this nourishing thread as is the fellowship meal of heaven when we have all been brought safely home. The parable of the Prodigal Son ends with the father throwing a party for the lost son who returned to safety, a celebration which the child who never left home refuses to attend because of jealousy and pride.

Unfortunately, it becomes clear that God has the same

problems as we do when we decide to put on any event and make a general invitation to all our acquaintances to attend. We wonder first how many people will turn up and then how they will behave themselves when they get inside.

In my village we run a music festival and over the years I've learned a lot about publicity and what you can expect as a return for your advertising budget. Once, I put on what I thought was a young rock band with a great future and I became so convinced that there would be crowds of unruly teenagers that I persuaded the organising committee to book some security guards. Of course, in the event, about twenty people turned up - for some reason, it's always about twenty - and the ones who came behaved very well. Even if people say they are coming to your function, you will never know for sure until they set foot in the door. Facebook has a facility where you can create an event and invite people and they can say that they intend to be present but even if two hundred people profess their eagerness to show they care about your invitation, you may still end up with your faithful twenty. On the other hand, funnily enough (and this is very biblical - think of the parable of the two sons asked to work in the fields) those who don't reply to your invitation may still come and they may even feel free to trash your place in return for your kindness.

It's comforting to know that God has the same problems about getting people to attend his event and about how people will behave if they come. Jesus talks about the behaviour issue first and says that some people attend the Kingdom banquet thinking it's somehow all about them. A colleague in ministry told me some time ago that virtually every problem people have either with receiving God's grace or living it out is to do with pride. Here is that uncomfortable reality in picture form at the great banquet. If you come to God's feast thinking you deserve a high place, then you should prepare yourself for a shock because it's very likely that someone you don't rate very highly is going to be on the top table. So, you'd might as well get used to putting others before yourself down here on earth.

The bigger problem is to get the people who have been invited to turn up in the first place and in the context, this is all about the Pharisees, those prime candidates for the liberation that is in Christ. They desperately wanted to please God and their hopes and dreams were standing realised in front of them in Jesus who was trying to usher them in to the feast of fulfilment. They still wouldn't come in.

The picture changes, this time likening God to a mother hen wanting to gather a gang of chicks who won't cooperate. For God, trying to gather in his beloved children must be like the proverbial herding of cats. The excuses people ever give! One has bought a field and has to go and see it even though, obviously, you don't buy a field you've never seen. Another has to try out the oxen he's just bought, as if somehow you'd buy a used car without a test drive. One is getting married. Well, some people always do have a valid reason not to attend your party, although if I were getting married I'd be more than happy to go through the ceremony and then attend the biggest wedding reception of time and eternity to celebrate - especially if someone else was paying.

Is there anything wrong? (Luke 14:15-24)
The people who end up going to God's wedding feast are the poor, the lame, the blind, the crippled and a rabble from the ends of the earth. Maybe Jesus just wants to upset people when he says this and is trying to shock the complacent and respectable into changing their minds about rejecting his invitation.

There is a lot in the Old Testament to suggest that disabled people can have no part in God's service - the priest and the worshippers in the Temple had to be physically perfect as did even the animals to be sacrificed - so to think that in God's presence at the end, good religious people will be shut out while those regarded as imperfect outsiders come in is hard to swallow. I read today of a Turkish couple who gave food to Syrian refugees rather than to their guests on their wedding day. Luke's story of inclusion is as astonishing as that.

Disabled people have always been hard done by and never more so than where there's a religious stigma attached. We remember the enquiries of the crowds and even the disciples about why people are born with impediments – perhaps, goes the theory, they sinned in some former life or maybe their parents were hiding some dark secret. Jesus rejects this attitude out of hand but it didn't stop people thinking it privately and it doesn't prevent the thought from crossing people's minds even today.

Jesus challenged the fact that disabled people were shut out of the Temple by carrying out healings in the very courts of the holy place but his language when talking about the Great Banquet of God's presence is still surprising.

Maybe Jesus is painting a picture of the diversity to be found in God's family. Let them all come in! We do know that around the throne of God will be a multitude no one could count and that it will include people from every imaginable grouping but all the same the vocabulary of poverty and disability is a strange one to reach for to describe diversity. It sounds more like the language of minority and difference than that of vast and broad inclusion.

Perhaps what we are dealing with is an image of spiritual healing - after all, our hymn books would be empty if we couldn't sing, 'Hear him, you deaf, his praise, you dumb, your loosened tongues employ' or 'I once was blind but now I see.' I think, though, that if I were disabled in any of the ways mentioned in our songs, I'd be upset to have an integral aspect of my personality used as an image of spiritual death in this way. Once, I had to challenge a leader in my church who was talking about the Paralympics and again and again was talking about people, 'who have something wrong with them.' I think immediately of a current hero of mine, the American musician Rachel Flowers. I first saw her in an internet video playing the amazingly complex progressive rock music of Emerson Lake and Palmer first on the piano, then on the organ. At first, I was astounded that one so young could achieve what she had (she was about sixteen at the time) but, after a while, it dawned on me that she is blind. There is nothing wrong with Rachel Flowers.

I think it is more like this: Jesus, or Luke the gospel writer (or Jesus as described by Luke) is interested in disabled people and is passionate about making them whole. That is already clear in what I called the Overture to the gospel, the song of Mary we know as the Magnificat. God is compassionate towards those in our society who need help and who are people of value in spite of all the obstacles society puts in their way. Examples of those on whom Jesus had mercy even in the early chapters of Luke are too numerous to list but already I've written about a leper, a woman with a flow of blood, the raising of a widow's son and many more. We know from bitter experience, though, that not all are physically healed in this way today.

I'm a great fan of the singer Robert Wyatt who was a rock and jazz drummer with Soft Machine and Matching Mole before being paralysed after falling from a window in 1973. His career since then has been interesting - there's a vulnerability in his singing voice and a toughness in his outlook, particularly in his politics that both excite me in different ways. In 1974, Wyatt had a completely unexpected hit single with a cover of The Monkees hit 'I'm a believer' and the story goes that the producers of the British pop music show 'Top of the Pops' did all they could to prevent him appearing on television in a wheelchair for fear of somehow upsetting the viewers. Fortunately, they didn't succeed.

Things are very different today because we rightly go to tremendous lengths to make sure that all facilities are available to disabled people but I know that plenty of things still need to be modified in terms of our practice and our attitudes. Recently, I went to see Shakespeare's 'Merchant of Venice' in Stratford-upon-Avon and I was expecting special insight on the alleged anti-semitic emphasis of the play, what with a Palestinian actor playing Shylock. In the end, though, it was a disabled actor in a minor role who challenged me about my degree of acceptance. I know it shouldn't really matter but I kept on thinking about her in my response to the performance and concluded that it must have been an intentional piece of casting in a work about difference.

We are thinking about the Great Banquet and the invitation

Jesus makes to all to come in. In the context, he longs for the Pharisees who are striving in all kinds of sincere but misguided ways to find a way around the simplicity of the grace of faith. These prime candidates for admission to the feast write themselves out of the story by opposition and foolish excuses to do in the end with materialism and the heavy responsibilities of family life. Even those who do come to the banquet are so often thinking that God's celebration is all about their personal virtue rather than about his free welcome of other people. The tables will be filled not with the self-righteous but with a grateful rabble from the four points of the compass along with the poor, the lame, the blind. Even if for some reason we think of many of them as outsiders, foreigners and aliens now, we won't then: we will see clearly not only that they are our brothers and sisters now but that they were all along. As for the disabled, they certainly won't have 'something wrong with them' in the fullness of God's presence.

Welcome Home (Luke 15:11-32)
It was Oscar Wilde who said that, 'Every saint has a past, and every sinner has a future.' The parable of the Prodigal Son shows a young man enthusiastically constructing a dreadful past before he comes to his senses. It's a tale of astonishing power. One of my enduring memories is of reading it with a group of homeless men and women in France: it was their story and the hush that fell on the room while it

was being told will live with me for ever.

There's always more to be said about this magnificent passage and there are many ways into it via the three main characters - a father and two sons. This time, I find myself wondering how the father was feeling when the younger son came to ask for his share of the family inheritance. Maybe he was shocked because, after all, to ask for your legacy before your parent has died is as much as to say that you are looking forward to their death. Nonetheless, I like to think that the father was optimistic about what his child could achieve if given his chance to prove himself. Perhaps we think of Paul in 1 Corinthians 13 who told us that, 'love always trusts and always hopes.' Surely most fathers believe their offspring have it in them to do well.

One of the problems with this parable is that we know it so well that nothing can surprise us about it any longer. We know that the prodigal turned out to be a fool with his money but we shouldn't lose sight of him striding away from the family home with a light step and full pockets. He didn't set out to ruin everything and throw it all away; he wanted to set the world on fire and maybe return some time as a successful man with riches of his own. We never do set out to spoil our lives.

Much of the story is about the far country and the way things went wrong for the younger son and perhaps we don't need to dwell too much on that because nearly all of us have been around the block.

I don't suppose for most of us our lives have unfolded in quite the way we hoped and expected when we picked up that suitcase and consulted the bus timetable for the far country. Experience has a way of changing us. Another Bible passage about fathers, this time one about God himself in his role as our heavenly guardian vividly tells us that we need to be disciplined in life. For many of us, the dreams of a great future that we see in our own children bring a wistful smile as we think of all the opportunities and choices that narrowed down to the life we actually find ourselves leading. We are older and, we hope, wiser.

The Prodigal is very busy as he wastes all his resources, plunging under his own weight about as far as it was possible to fall in terms of the Judaism of his day - namely by having to take a job feeding someone else's pigs. The footballer George Best brilliantly described the kind of purposeful wastefulness that must have taken place: 'I spent a lot of money on booze, birds and fast cars. The rest I just squandered.'

Eventually, the younger son 'came to his senses' - he literally 'came to himself'. This is a very suggestive phrase and this is no time to engage in the kind of theological speculation encouraged by other parts of the New Testament in a rarefied atmosphere where we are encouraged to wonder whether human beings are divided into two parts or three. Perhaps we are soul and body, or maybe we are body, soul and spirit - who knows? I certainly don't. It's good to spend time in the gospels because here we see people being made whole as whatever different parts of us there may be are integrated and are no longer warring against each other but instead are brought together in harmonious interaction. When Jesus heals the person who is possessed by a legion of demons, the poor man is, for the first time in ages, 'in his right mind' just as the younger son has 'come to himself.'

All the same, the Prodigal had still lost everything and so much had been spoiled. The best he could hope for is . . . Well, let's hear him express it himself in the words of the sad homecoming speech he composed as he trudged back: 'How many of my father's hired servants have food to spare, and here I am starving to death! I will set out and go back to my father and say to him: Father, I have sinned against heaven and against you. I am no longer worthy to be called your son; make me like one of your hired servants.' What he expects from his father is reproach and a life of payback.

In an amazing turnaround, we realise that while the runaway has been frantically hurling money into the gutter, the father has been active, too. I portrayed him hoping for the best as he waved goodbye, but that was speculation. On the other hand, Jesus explicitly tells us he is watching all the time that the son is away, finally running out and embracing the returning rebel, ignoring his carefully memorised words of repentance, commanding a feast to be prepared and finally pleading with the son who stayed at home to join in the joy of the household.

This overwhelming expression of free grace with no strings attached is difficult for some to take. For instance, Saint Augustine - a man who knew more than a little about the prodigal life - felt that penitence must be explicit and reparation should be made. It is true that we should take the consequences of our rebellion seriously but this is perilously close to the thinking of the elder son who never left home and who resents his brother's return. For the moment the father is so overwhelmed with love and relief that he isn't concerned with accountancy. Even though he gave no speech of shame, the Prodigal received, according to the symbolism of the time, with a robe the restored honour of the son; with a ring the renewed authority of the son; with shoes the restored freedom of the son.

A great gulf fixed (Luke 16:19-31)

Like the Good Samaritan and the Prodigal Song, the story of the rich man and Lazarus is only to be found in Luke's gospel. We know because he tells us so that Luke searched out other sources than those available to the other evangelists for his version of the life and teaching of Jesus and we are grateful that he did because he came across gems of great human interest. In fact, these tales are so vivid that they are probably the best-known parts of the teaching of Jesus.

There has been a lot of debate about whether what I am going to call 'Dives and Lazarus' is a factual account or a parable. Usually, parables are flagged up as such in the text and they are often short and grouped together but this one stands alone and is presented as an insight with an unusual amount of detail into how things are after the death of the main characters.

Maybe this story is an original one by Jesus or perhaps he inherited it - it certainly sounds like a folk tale so I tend to agree with scholars who think it is inspired by Jewish sources and is a parable rather than a depiction of real events in the hereafter: there is a long tradition of storytelling to make a point in Judaism. Whatever opinion we favour, anyone can see that it's a good story well told and with a moral that is very clear and that leads to a call to action that is uniquely compelling.

As far as the names Dives and Lazarus are concerned, Lazarus means 'leper' but it is also, of course, the name of the man in John's gospel brought back from the dead by Jesus. Dives simply means, 'rich man' in Latin but the narrative is so vivid that it almost requires you to assign names to the characters so 'Dives and Lazarus' it is.

The details of the story have suggested many works of art and were even the conscious inspiration for a lot of Victorian social enterprises which so often depended on the trickle down of wealth from rich to poor. I can't imagine it having a similar effect outside the church today, though, because nowadays we seem pretty well shameless in our pursuit of a luxury that would make even Dives feel like a pauper. Even within the community of faith we can't always be said to have escaped this spirit of the age.

So, I think this is a parable rather than a depiction of real events in the afterlife. I don't know what Abraham's bosom might be and I wonder why particular prominence should be given to Abraham except that he often features as the great figure of inclusion in Luke's gospel - the man of faith before the community of the Law was established. All the same, there is a great debate in Christianity at the moment about the reality of hell and eternal punishment and it often references the Dives and Lazarus story. Prominent evangelicals are openly speculating about the temporary nature of any punishment there might be and wonder whether even if hell is real it might stand empty as a testimony to the saving power of God through the work of Christ.

For what it's worth, my own view is that the Bible clearly teaches a system of rewards and punishments based on a last and decisive judgement but that the Christian has no need to fear this assessment because of the cross. Crucially, though, our works and efforts will be evaluated and recognised for what they are and for the motives which led to them being done. In this context, I remember the apostle Paul's teaching that on the foundation of Christ's work we are all building either with wood, hay or stone and that we may be saved either as brands from the burning or tas the bearers of a crown. In any case, the quality of what we have done will be known.

By now, anybody reading this post will know there are many questions to be asked of this passage. Just for the sake of completeness, I will mention Abraham's words to Dives about a resurrection from the dead. I don't think this is a prophecy of the rising of Christ from the dead, although I do think Luke would expect his readers to pick up on the reference with the benefit of hindsight.

Whatever answers are given to these many queries, the teaching of the parable is clear and twofold. First, we are meant to learn that any prosperity we may enjoy in this life is literally temporary - of the moment - and does not relate to what eternity may have in store for us. Our plenty can be snatched away in an instant and give way to a shocking new set of realities altogether. The parable of the rich fool is a clear parallel with Dives and Lazarus and both passages are meant to teach us that our relationship to this world, its goods and rewards is meant to be a light one and one we can leave at the shortest of short notice.

The second clear point to come out of the story of Dives and Lazarus is that the plight of the poor is before us day and night and we are responsible for helping those we can. Why they are in poverty is not revealed to us in this story but God's fatherly concern for them certainly is and it is obvious that how we react to their presence in our midst has a bearing on how we will be greeted by God after death. There are scholarly questions about the text and about details of its interpretation but the most important question of all is quite unambiguous. It asks us what we are going to do about those in need today. If, by being born when we were born in the affluent West, we have won first prize in the lottery of life, then what we do here on earth should testify to our gratitude as we strive to store up treasures in heaven.

Wade in the water (Luke 17:11-19)

When I was about twelve years old, I went out collecting door-to-door to raise money to fight leprosy. The invitation we were told to give was that it only cost some derisory sum to cure someone of this dreadful disease which even today disfigures people and divides families and communities, destroying livelihoods and self-esteem as it advances. I still wonder why as a world community we don't just stump up the money and wipe out this scourge.

In Hebrew, the word for a leper comes from a root to do with being struck a blow by someone. At the time of Jesus it was certainly taken for granted that a sufferer had been singled out by God for special attention in this way. There is plenty of encouragement for that notion in the Old Testament where leprosy is often used as a metaphor for the sin that disfigures and separates us, making us hate ourselves and others in the process. Maybe that's why many commentators think that in Isaiah 53 the Suffering Servant of the Lord may have been smitten with leprosy. The prophet tells us that the punishment that brings us peace is on this mysterious figure but we wrongly thought God hated him. This description fits very well with an Old Testament interpretation of what was going on when someone stopped being a person and became merely a leper instead.

The ten lepers in Luke's gospel knew their condition was hopeless and that their best bet was to stick together. They knew it was pointless for them to go to the priest for comfort because it would be his duty simply to confirm their condition and enforce their exclusion. Even doctors at that time were unable to help and no amount of compassionate nursing would make things better in the long term.

Jesus was passing by, though, and that detail is important because a glance at the geography of this part of the gospel shows that he didn't have to travel the way he was going through these biblical badlands. He takes an inconvenient detour to help these lepers because of his love and also because there are important lessons in what he will do and say during the encounter. It's encouraging to know that Jesus always happens to be passing even today, going out of his way to meet us in our wandering.

The ten pariahs did the best thing they could under the circumstances by crying out for help and using the best title for Jesus they knew at the time. The name 'Jesus' is a proper noun with a meaning - 'God saves' - but they didn't know his name, so their highest thought was to cry out to the Rabbi, the Master. It's a sobering thought that many of us are experts in listing the names and titles of Jesus but we somehow forget to call out to him for help in spite of our great knowledge and our lofty conceptions.

The lepers were cured by following the instructions of Jesus to go and show themselves to the priest, an action which would in the normal course of events have only confirmed their condemnation to exile. It was while they were on the way of obedience that they were healed by God.

The parallel with Naaman in the Old Testament is clear and will have escaped no one in Luke's readership who was steeped in the text and telling of the Bible. This captain of the Syrian army was cured of his leprosy by taking the prophet Elisha at his word and going to wash seven times in the river Jordan. I understand from people who have been there that the Jordan is a disappointing river for the tourist and that there are far better sights even in that part of the world but this unassuming stretch of water represents so much to us because of the Bible events that take place in an around it. For Naaman, to wash there was God's designated way of healing even though there were better rivers elsewhere, as he himself testily points out.

There were many more spectacular actions of religious devotion that Naaman could have contrived but he was purified as he washed, just as the lepers were cleansed as they went. For our part, when we find out what God wants, our best course is to do it. When I preached on this passage, I made an application here to do with baptism and wondered aloud when it was that the united testimony of the Bible and the Church of all ages stopped being enough to convince people of the need to be baptised and when it was that the feelings and preferences of the individual became the deciding factor. I'm still wondering, but it is so.

It's obvious that all ten lepers were very glad to have been healed and to see the disfigurement vanish from their own skin and that of their companions. Nine out of ten of them just got on with their lives, though, maybe with not many lessons learned from the episode of sickness. Just one of them was so grateful to God that he thought to turn back and seek out Jesus to thank him in person. I'm not doing a lot of preaching at the moment but old habits die hard and I can't resist pointing out that a thankful heart is a surprisingly rare commodity these days even though our many blessings are not our due, or just good luck, or written in the stars but free gifts from a gracious God.

There is a punchline to this story as there so often is in Luke's way of telling the stories. Once again, it's a sucker punch: the thankful leper was, shock horror, a Samaritan. This detail, insignificant for us, is the whole point of the tale. Yet again, it's impossible for me to convey the shock of the s-word unless I start implying that as you are reading this, you are a racist, and I won't do that. I do ask you, though, to make a huge effort of the imagination and wonder how it would be if there were someone you looked down on or disliked for some reason - someone you've written out of your life. Yes, I know it's hard and there's probably nobody who's in this category but do try, please.

By mentioning that the grateful leper was a Samaritan, this story says that God loves even that person and showers graces on them just as he does on you. We shouldn't assume that God withholds his goodness from those we don't rate very highly. Maybe we should swallow our pride and tell them about God's mercy. We may find they turn out to be even more thankful to God than we are ourselves as we go on our way without a second thought.

God is an unjust judge (Luke 18:1-8)
I don't think I'm giving too much away if I say there's a hidden key to the Baptist chapel in the village where I live. I was surprised to discover that one of the most faithful leaders of the church who was

here long before I came and who constantly needs access to the building didn't know about it but, on reflection, I suppose it's good for only a few members to be in on the secret. After all, there wouldn't be any point in hanging a key by the front door with a notice drawing attention to it.

Luke chapter 18 starts with two parables with the key in full view by the entrance and with a big sign in block capitals pointing to it. The second one, the story of the Pharisee and the tax collector is a direct challenge to those who feel worthy to stand before God but who look down on others: it teaches us about humility in our approach to the Lord and warns the presumptuous to take a good long look at themselves.

The first story gives advice we may think is not worth giving - that we should always pray and not give up. We all know we should pray and that we should probably be more persistent in making time to do so. All the same, I was struck when reading an anthology of short essays on prayer by prominent Christian leaders - archbishops, writers on the spiritual life and the like - that they practically all began with some form of disclaimer that they weren't experts in the matter at all and I wondered what hope there was for me. Time constraints, discouragement, lack of faith, pride, sin, wrong conceptions of God and ourselves, all these factors militate against our prayer life.

A good place to start to encourage a healthy approach to prayer is to get our view of God sorted out, and that's where this chapter begins when Jesus tells us about a judge who doesn't care about people and has no respect for his maker, the source of his authority. We are meant to come up with a jolt against this description. We know the story is about God and we are shocked that he should be described in this way, so everything we know already about our heavenly Father revolts against the suggestion that he could ever be unjust, callous and indifferent to need. You know God does care about justice and is grieved that the world is in the state it is and you are aware that the story of the Fall in Genesis depicts the collapse of the ideal relationship between the world and the creator. You are aware, too, that he has put into practice a plan to put things right by the coming of Christ and that there will be a glorious conclusion when joy and restoration reign. In the meantime, you are confident that God weeps over the individual victims of poverty, misery and lies. Your experience of God shows that he cares about you and in your best moments you love to sing about it: 'Great is thy faithfulness, O God my Father.' So, your hackles should rise at the suggestion even in the mouth of Jesus that God is like an unjust judge. Sometimes you feel, like Abraham pleading for Sodom, that you could pray and reason with God to act in a way befitting his character of mercy.

The parable is not only about an unjust judge but also involves a persistent widow with whom we are meant to identify as we come to prayer. The recommendation is that we should lay siege to God's presence and refuse to depart without the blessing. At the height of our faith, we are not only like pleading Abraham but like wrestling Jacob, too. Jesus says that type of approach is going to work even with a corrupt official who doesn't care about justice and is indifferent to people so it is bound to have results with a Father who loves what is right and has a parental regard for all the people he has made.

    I don't know enough about this aspect of prayer and yet I have known something of it in the past. The manna of yesterday doesn't nourish today, though, and I need to gather fresh stores even now as I write. One of the most precious times in my ministry was also one of the most testing when a young and strong aspiring tennis professional in a church in France fell ill with cancer and was thought unlikely to recover. I felt, rightly or wrongly, that he was taking this crushing news too easily and that he must have serious questions about God's provision that he wasn't telling me about. Even as a young and inexperienced minister, I directed him to some Psalms in the seventies and eighties of that compendium of human experience - the ones where people have a controversy with their maker and ask him with passion to come clean about what is going on. God did marvellous things in that situation, in the young man's life of faith and in that of his family and of the wider church fellowship. There were baptisms, marriages, reconciliation and healing through medicine that we were all able to witness with wonder.

This first parable of the chapter shows that God can easily endure a direct and honest approach on the part of his children. Obviously, there are problems here to do with our conception of our Father in heaven and regarding the rest of the Bible's teaching on prayer. We are told by Jesus elsewhere that God knows what we need before we ask so maybe we wonder why we should need to bring anything to him at all. Maybe we wonder why there is so often a delay in his answer and why there is a need for persistence at all. Clearly, I don't have any easy answers to questions like those although I suspect they have to do with the way God's different types of providence interact, now directing such and such a thing to happen while preventing such and such another from taking place. Nonetheless, whatever our understanding of these things, the teaching of the parable is clear and it is that we are to be constant in prayer - 'Oh, what peace we often forfeit, oh what needless pain we bear all because we do not carry everything to God in prayer.'

The chapter begins with the disciples and with Jesus telling them they should pray and not give up. There's a bitter irony here because the outline of the cross is beginning to loom on the horizon in these chapters and we know in hindsight that the teaching of the Master was in vain in this instance and that these followers would first fall asleep in the Garden of Gethsemane and then turn tail and run from the crisis. The story ends in an unusual place - with the doubt of Jesus. That's an extraordinary thought, but Jesus wonders aloud whether when he returns he will find his latter day disciples faithful in prayer or not and whether this aspect of things will be thrilling or disappointing to him when he comes back. I suppose the answer to that is up to each of us.

Do I hear a waltz? (Luke 18:9-14)
In the second of the parables at the start of Luke 18 there are two men, one happy, outgoing and confident and one deeply upset and very inward. In spite of appearances to the contrary, they are both in serious danger: they have come into God's presence, after all. To go to the Temple was to appear where the glory of God dwelt. People become casual about the reality of God who is deeper than our breathing and closer than the air but the Old Testament is full of incidents to warn us that you don't just waltz into an audience with him.

Once, in the time of King David, they were bringing the ark of the covenant to Jerusalem with the latest technology for transport in the form of a new cart as opposed to the poles that should have been used to carry it. The ark tottered and a man called Ahio fell dead as he impulsively reached out his hand to steady it. On another occasion, when Elijah challenged the prophets of Baal, they discovered that God is a consuming fire as well as a still, small voice. The prophet Isaiah who is, if we are to read his book in chronological order, a self-confident and critical man at the beginning of his career, sees God's glory and he changes in an instant to become more malleable and compassionate as he dies to himself. Ezekiel had a vision of God and fell at the Lord's feet like a dead man, only to rise as a mighty spokesman for the Lord - but only from then on. The Bible tells us that no one has seen God and lived to tell the tale but fortunately there are many instances of those for whom to appreciate his reality was a life-changing experience.

The first man Jesus describes is, once again, a Pharisee and he doesn't give much of an impression of being in danger at all in his encounter with God. He is full of self-confidence and his words are systematically self-adoring as he spreads out before God a list of his admirable abstentions and his awesome observances while informing the Lord that he is a wonderful specimen of spiritual rectitude. There's a remarkable little expression in the parable when Jesus tells us that, 'he prayed about himself' or, in an alternative translation, that 'he prayed within himself.' His prayers obviously get no higher than his fat, proud head as he communes not with the Lord of the universe but with his own pride. Thank goodness religious people don't behave like that today - Church life would be so awful if they did.

Even though we shouldn't fall into the trap of sitting in

judgement on the Pharisee, we can see that he commits fatal error after fatal error and probably the worst is deciding to compare himself favourably with the tax collector. As soon as you begin to sit as a judge over other people, you put yourself in spiritual jeopardy because Jesus tells us that the same measure you use with other people will be used with you. Even the Lord's prayer contains the petition, 'Forgive us our trespasses as we forgive those who trespass against us' - a request which asks that equal mercy be shown to us all.

The second man is a tax collector and he is clearly in grave danger for a number of reasons as he approaches the Lord. His job is one that practically always involved corruption and collaboration with the occupying forces of Rome and, therefore, a degree of treachery to the people of God. His attitude is cringing and dramatically self-abasing and in fact many would say it is a little too demonstrative for comfort what with the breast-beating. Whatever we think about his behaviour, though, what he says is pure gold for anyone who is interested in coming close to the creator in safety: 'God, be merciful to me, a sinner'.

Of these two men in danger, most observers would make an easy assessment. One is a fine, upstanding religious man while the other is a snivelling wreck, broken with guilt and compromised by his job. Our criteria are often the wrong ones because we forget that, 'People look at the outward appearance but God looks on the heart'.

Anyway, what really matters in this type of situation is not our opinion of others or even of ourselves. God's evaluation of us is so important that nothing else matters in the slightest.

The parable contains the important Bible word 'justified' which speaks of being declared right with God and acceptable to him. It is very much like Luke in his gospel to include among the people declared righteous before the Lord someone who would be shut out by everyone else. It is very like Jesus, too. 'My song is love unknown, my Saviour's love to me: love to the loveless shown that they might lovely be,' as the seventeenth century cleric Samuel Crossman puts it in his beautiful hymn.

Thinking about this parable, I find myself wondering what may have happened afterwards. It's pointless to speculate really but in a way Jesus encourages us in this direction when he says the tax collector didn't just leave the Temple justified but went home in that state. Maybe it's not too daring to imagine that the Pharisee will have returned home still unaware of his danger and bent on keeping up his life of ostentatious piety until, after death, he found himself trying to pay an infinite debt with the coppers of an obsolete currency. This is not to judge him but to point out the logical conclusion of self-absorption. Anyway, perhaps God encountered him in a dramatic way before it was too late.

The question is a little more complicated about the tax

collector. He was justified by God because he had been realistic about his danger and called for mercy but his visit to the Temple hadn't helped him from a human point of view. He had only found himself used as a cautionary tale in the prayer of a religious success story and hadn't actually received any outward encouragement from God. I imagine, though, a certain lightness of spirit and some kind of joy invading him as he returns to his place with an inward sense that all is right between himself and God. Now, of course, he has a problem in that he still has to earn a living as a tax collector but Barclay helps us yet again by telling us that there was a statue in those days to 'The Fair Tax Collector' - a rare figure indeed but not unknown. The suggestion is that there exists a way of doing even what we have to do from necessity in a right and honourable way.

The key to this second parable in Luke 18 is again at the door in full view. The first story of the widow and the unjust judge tells us to pray and not give up, even though Jesus himself is doubtful whether his words will be taken to heart by his followers. This time, the tale is told to instruct us not to trust in what we see as our own qualities when we come to God. There is no waltzing in as far as he is concerned; we need his mercy, each and every one of us.

The baby place (Luke 18:15-30)

We all need to rely on so many things to be able to flourish or even survive: we can't do without food and shelter and even friends and family can hardly be described as a luxury. It is good to be able to count on law and order or healthcare, although so many in the world have to do without them. When you were a baby you had to have an absolute reliance on someone to feed you, keep you safe and give you the affirmation without which we are told infants will languish. It is tragic when all these are unavailable for whatever reason or when they go wrong either because of weakness or wickedness. When we are very old, the situation may well be similar and many of us will need the help of others as we prepare ourselves to come to God. In the middle years of strength and vigour we still find ourselves leaning on something or someone. In these verses from Luke 18, Jesus performs a very beautiful action and then draws a teaching from it about reliance before a man appears right on cue to illustrate exactly what Jesus is saying.

I began this book on 'Luke, Stranger' by saying that religion historically has practically always been a power game with men as the main players and money as the playing chips. I said that it's a story about domination, violence and exploitation in which even children who ought to be protected are often put at risk and even taught to fight.

The real, invisible kingdom of God is not like that at all. When some mothers brought babies to Jesus to be blessed by him, the disciples tried in a display of macho power to deny them access to the master but Jesus welcomed them and told his would-be protectors that we all need to receive the kingdom like children. I take him to mean that just as babies come into the world with nothing and are totally reliant on others for every detail of their young lives, so we should recognise that all we will ever receive spiritually comes from God.

This is a hard saying for some of us who feel we've battled hard for any progress we have made in the spiritual life and want to protect jealously any ground we have gained. This is a wrong attitude: a baby needs regular feeding and we in our turn need daily nourishment from God rather than a stockpile of rotting food we've gathered ourselves and kept for consumption at some indeterminate time in the future.

Next, we meet in the flesh rather than in a parable one of those poor hapless people who come to Jesus bloated with their worldly capital and who leave punctured and leaking all over the scenery. What a build-up: he is a ruler, a rich man and righteous. He gives every appearance of being a winner who is politically influential, has social standing and a financial security that means he is immune from the nagging fear many endure that the bottom could drop out economically at any moment. He reminds me of the apostle Paul in his second letter to the Corinthians or the one to the Philippians when he begins to make a satirical list of all his many qualities only to say they are dross and worthless when compared with his knowledge of Christ.

There is something lacking in the life of this rich ruler and he knows it only too well. All our securities, these pensions, possessions and positions, can make us unusually fearful about losing them - at least as long as the fundamental question about eternal life remains unresolved. When we stand before God without our houses and cars and with no financial plan and reputation, what then?

Jesus is harsh with this enquirer but we have to suppose he is being cruel to be kind, otherwise he's teaching us at the expense of another human being with dignity and I don't think Jesus would ever do that. We have to suppose that when Jesus talks about selling goods and distribution to the poor, he is correct in his diagnosis that this man's security is not in God but in his wealth. And - we fervently hope just for the moment - this rich ruler is unable to accept what Jesus says and goes away sad.

Such a conversation puzzles the disciples because they assume that worldly goods are a sign of God's favour on someone. Of course, possessions can act in this way but at the same time they always lead to a test of herculean proportions: we know that not many of us can be entrusted with wealth and influence without falling under their spell.

In the parable of the sower one of the sets of seeds is choked to death by just this danger as the type of person represented in the parallelism has any relationship with God wrested away.

Near the start of my ministry, I read a great book called 'Money and Power' by the French writer Jacques Ellul - 'Money, Sex and Power' by the American Quaker Richard Foster is better-known in the English-speaking world but is heavily influenced by Ellul. I guess the default position on power for most of us is based on the famous saying of Lord Acton that 'power corrupts and absolute power corrupts absolutely.' Our feelings about money are less straightforward: probably most people think of it as being morally neutral and we feel that it is the use people make of money that counts. Long ago, I was intrigued to find that Ellul does not teach that at all and bases his thinking on the fact that money is the second most common topic in the spoken ministry of Jesus after the connected subject of the Kingdom of God. For the French writer, money has a personality and he takes seriously the fact that Jesus even gives it a name: Mammon. In the quaint expression of the Puritans, Mammon has a tendency to 'take us off from God.' According to Ellul, we must not be passive in our attitude to money but instead confront and deny its power over us and forcibly place it in God's Kingdom.

That type of thinking would have been news to the disciples and it is not very familiar today in a church where prosperity teaching has been allowed to spread its ridiculous lies all too widely. It's a safe bet, though, that wherever we are in our spiritual life there are personal or impersonal forces trying to drag us backwards and one of those may well be money or what it can buy.

As usual, Peter puts his foot in it, albeit in a more subtle way than usual. He does this by showing in what he says that his security is not in Jesus himself but in the act of having followed Jesus. That's a fine distinction, so let's be charitable and say that his foot is not wholly inserted into his mouth but is instead making a tentative step away from it and in the right direction. After all, at least his security is not in riches or influence. Faith in faith itself is not faith in God, though, and to renounce possessions is not necessarily to accept Christ's lordship.

Jesus tells his disciples to find their security in following God. Somehow or another, we all need to find the way of the young child and be reliant on God for everything. Fortunately, what is almost incredibly difficult for a human being is possible for God who is able to bring us safely through to his presence. We badly need to be in the 'baby place' of reliance on God.

Starman (Luke 19:1-10)

When we lost David Bowie a few years back, one of the best things I saw by way of tribute celebrated his humour rather than his massive and diverse contribution to world culture. It was a brief extract from the Ricky Gervais series 'Extras'. Ricky portrays a struggling actor who has managed to get some measure of cheap success in a sitcom that even he can see is vulgar and degrading but it least it has given him the opportunity to catch a glimpse of Bowie in a VIP hospitality area at some function. Gervais sits down casually and once he has managed to explain to the singer who he is, he tries to get sympathy by complaining about the appallingly low standards of the general public. Bowie is only half-listening but then he goes over to a piano and, in a moment of inspiration, starts improvising a song: 'Pathetic little fat man, national joke.' Everybody stops making cocktail conversation and starts to listen and by the end, to the discomfiture of Ricky Gervais, they are all singing along: 'See his pug-nosed face. Pug, pug. Pug, pug.'

In the last section, 'The baby place', I wrote about a rich ruler with reputation, standing and resources but lacking a sense of security with God. Jesus looks at him with love and tells him to sell everything he has to become a true follower. The secure establishment figure is unable to comply and goes away sad, we hope just for a time. After all, Jesus always provides the strength to fulfil what he demands.

Shortly after this episode, there is an illustration of what answering the call of Jesus in the affirmative might look like. It takes place in Jericho - a god-forsaken place where, according to the Bible prohibition, no one should have built anything after the destruction of the city at the time of the conquest under Joshua. Cities are tenacious, though, and land is too valuable to go to waste, so there is by the time of Jesus a thriving community there. One of its inhabitants is a man called Zacchaeus who is not only a tax-collector but a chief tax-collector, if you please. We are told he was rich but really that goes without saying in the world of the gospels where, for the taxman, corruption was part of the job and from a human point of view you probably couldn't make ends meet without it.

I told the story about David Bowie and Ricky Gervais because I imagine something similar happening with Zacchaeus who is, in this situation, just a small man up a tree struggling to keep his balance. It would have been easy, with the cover of the anonymity of the crowd waiting for Jesus, to start up a chant about the local swindler. As Jesus passes through the town, he looks up and sees Zacchaeus, decides to call him down and invites himself round for a meal, to the general indignation of the onlookers who will have known what kind of unregenerate sinner Zacchaeus is and will probably have been exploited by him on a regular basis.

Once, I was asked by a church in the southern suburbs of Paris to keep a market stall selling Bibles. I was asking for volunteers to help in this thankless task, which involved setting up in the dark early morning in winter and then standing there while people rushed by looking for food, so I was grateful when a young man came forward to offer his services. Several people came up to me later and wrote him off with the words, *Il n'est pas intéressant* - 'he is not interesting, he is a waste of space.' Shame on them: no one is ever written off by Jesus, at least not while they are still alive and can be brought to faith and amendment of life.

I wonder how Jesus knew about Zacchaeus even as far as knowing him by name. Maybe it was because of supernatural knowledge, or perhaps the chant of the crowd I have imagined really took place and told Jesus all he needed to know. John, in his gospel, tells us that Jesus doesn't have to ask about what is hidden in the recesses of character of a person because he knows already but a clue given by the insults and cries of the observers seem pretty likely to me, too.

We know from our own experience that Jesus never gives up on anyone and that it is in his nature and policy to keep on giving us the chance to change. For his part, Zacchaeus could have politely declined the invitation to come down but he recognises that, in his life as a marginalised outsider, this is the 'crisis of judgement for gain or for loss' that one of our hymns talks about. Whereas the rich ruler for all his advantages was unable to follow Jesus, Zaccaeus shins down his sycamore, shedding his wealth as he slides. Spontaneously, without even being challenged to it, he produces fruits worthy of repentance. In keeping with the teaching of Jacques Ellul on the personality of Mammon, he refuses its power and places his money in the Kingdom of God instead, acting with justice first and then with charity after all his obligations have been fulfilled.

Jesus concludes the incident by giving us the teaching of the gospel in two pithy sentences: 'Today, salvation has come to this house because this man, too, is a son of Abraham. For the Son of Man came to seek and to save the lost.' People like Zacchaeus are excluded from Judaism because of their corruption and collaboration but even those locked into these activities can come back into the holy family and enjoy table fellowship with Israel's Messiah.

A poor vintage (Luke 20:1-19)

For well over thirty years my preaching pattern was more or less the same for the time around Easter: I'd preach about Palm Sunday, then there'd be a Good Friday meditation and a celebration of the resurrection of Christ on Easter Sunday itself. There's nothing wrong with that practice because these events are the beating heart of the Christian faith and we do well to remember that as regularly as the heart itself beats.

I must say that I feel I have neglected the other events of what we call Passion Week, though, and because I've reached this point in Luke's gospel I thought I'd look at some of the things Jesus did and said between the time when he rode into Jerusalem in humble majesty and the time when he died on the cross.

The week starts with a massive show of force on the part of the Jewish establishment in response to the Palm Parade. All through the gospel they have been sending small delegations on missions into the far north around the Sea of Galilee to find out what is going on up there by spying on it. The inevitable disputes have been mainly about the rights and wrongs of healing on the Sabbath but now Jesus is in the headquarters of Judaism in the Temple itself and preaching the good news of a new awakening of the Kingdom of God not only in words but also in acted parables.

Jesus has entered Jerusalem in a way that clearly identifies him as the King of Israel foretold in the prophecy of Zechariah while the cleansing of the temple that closely follows that symbolic action is an open and contemptuous rejection of the marriage of money and religion that kept the economy of Jerusalem buoyant and buzzing. Maybe Jesus 'looking round' the temple on the evening of Palm Sunday is the formal inspection of a leprous house required by Leviticus while the cleansing is an acted parable of its cleansing.

On the part of the ruling authorities, there is no spying or discreet observation now: no more mister nice guy. This time, the chief priests, the teachers of the law and the elders come to question Jesus. There are at least six people, then, but a little bit of research and common sense suggests a much bigger group of critics. From the New Testament as a whole, we know the names of two of the priestly class called Annas and Caiaphas and of Gamaliel and Nicodemus, two of the elders, but we also see in John's gospel those among the elders strong enough to shout down the wavering but wakening Nicodemus and from the book of Acts those who would debate with the wise and cautious Gamaliel about the early Christian movement.

All this implies a sizeable group of hostile Jerusalem experts sent to put a stop to a movement from distant Galilee they think is laying siege to the centre. They see Jesus the Outsider as a successor of John the Baptist in bringing politically awkward strife. The gospels portray the Jewish authorities as terrified of making waves with the Romans. They had been unsure about John who had plenty to say to soldiers and taxmen and even to the puppet royalty. It is Jesus himself who throws the topic of the ministry of John the Baptist into the explosive mix and we know this was a controversial subject with two clearly-defined opinions being expressed about it: John's preaching and baptising was either divinely inspired or a merely human phenomenon. Jesus asks which opinion is favoured by the authorities.

Sometimes, an opinion is too dangerous to express. For instance, in the current refugee crisis in Europe, if a high-profile delegation came to me and asked if these poor people should be let into the United Kingdom or left to drown in the Mediterranean, I'd probably try to evade the question rather than leave myself open to the consequences of my choice (although, privately, I lean far more towards the option of allowing people to come here and settle). In the same way, after all due deliberation the authorities take refuge in a pompously resonant statement that always makes me laugh: 'We do not know.'

The correct answer to Jesus's question was that John the Baptist's ministry was an authentic breaking-in of the Kingdom of God into a long silence when prophecy had long since come to be seen as belonging firmly in the past. To hold that view on John, though, involves buying into God's unfolding plan of salvation in Christ. It means renouncing all chicanery and trickery and siding with the dangerous precariousness of God's ways in history.

Jesus then tells a story which is nothing less than an overarching interpretation of the long story of Israel, past, present and future. The vineyard in his parable is Israel itself seen as the prized possession of God, its owner. This is an image that goes back at least as far as the prophet Isaiah writing in the eighth century before Christ and even as far back as that it was already being used to highlight the striking contrast between the cherishing love God lavished on his winemaking project and the fruitlessness of the vine itself. So, Jesus highlights the shameful treatment God's messengers have seemingly always attracted in a religious setting where to speak on behalf of the deity is to be misunderstood, often wilfully. Moses, Samuel, Elijah, Elisha, Jeremiah and now John the Baptist were opposed to a man and the way their faithful testimony was disregarded constitutes the past of Israel seen as the vineyard.

By way of a final invitation to become involved in his story of salvation, God takes the audacious step of sending his own son to turn around the tale of denial and to fulfil all the prophecies of his spurned messengers in one go. This is an olive branch but, no: the institution and its fragile interface with the occupying powers, not to mention the personal authority of those in office could never be thrown away for the sake of faith in a carpenter on a donkey. This is the rational view which leads to the Passion Play of Easter week as the consequences of rejecting God's word about Israel the servant of the nations become first violent and then murderous. That is the present time in this story of the vineyard, the owner and the tenants.

The future is this: God, will break open the mould of Judaism as the Temple comes to be seen as a leprous house worthy only of the kind of destruction which is symbolised by the scourging cords of Christ as he overturns the tables. This symbolic ruination will be brought to reality by the besieging Roman armies in 70 AD.

God is telling the story and, as its climax, Jesus the Outsider will be vindicated by his raising from the dead when he will be given the name above every other name and declared Son of God with power. From now on, his kingdom will become a worldwide one and will just go on building and building.

The image Jesus uses to conclude his teaching on the history of Israel is once again an ancient one - that of the cornerstone - and one's attitude to this 'head of the corner' becomes a symbol of choice in the rest of the New Testament. According to Peter, whether as individuals or as a church, we will never be put to shame as long as we use that unique building block. For Paul, if we try to build on anything else in life or in the community of faith, we only waste our time. Instead, and unlike the Jerusalem authorities, we need to get on the right side of history.

Right on the money (Luke 20:20-26)
In the week leading up to the cross Jesus the Outsider has all kinds of individual parties and bizarre alliances within Judaism approach him as people who have little in common group together to oppose this interloper. On the occasion I'm looking at in this section, the Herodians and the Pharisees have an understanding as unlikely as a coalition between the Labour Party and the Conservatives in the United Kingdom or between the Republicans and the Democrats in the United States. The Pharisees in this group of spies would have firmly believed in opposing the Romans while the Herodians thought collaboration with the occupying force was the most constructive way

forward for the people. This is a fundamental point of difference but in opposition to Jesus two wildly differing factions found common ground. They came with a question about taxes and, when they asked if it was right to pay one's obligations to the occupying power, they were challenging Jesus to declare himself to be on one side or the other of their own great debate about the status of Rome among them.

Jesus asked his interrogators to show him a coin and it wasn't just any coin he asked for but a denarius. Representing, as it did, the amount a worker was given for a day's labour, this sum of money had great symbolic importance. 'A day's work for a day's pay' is such a good slogan that it can easily be seen that the denarius stands for our very selves as well as the daily activities we carry out to put bread on the table for ourselves and for those who count on us.

We can leave aside for the moment the fact that people who didn't believe in the authority of Caesar shouldn't really have been able to produce his coin - indeed, they made a big noise about not dirtying their hands with the currency of the invader. The coin itself tells a story, carrying as it does the image of Caesar with all that implies: there is massive authority and influence behind that tiny piece of metal. As for the person holding out the coin for Jesus to look at, he bears an image, too, and it is an image with even greater dignity than that of Caesar, because it is the image of God. In the hand of that accusing person, there are two competing allegiances. We have the same dilemma, bearing as we do the same two images in tension. We live in society and have obligations and privileges which stem from that belonging but God has stamped us with his likeness as well.

It's hard for us to opt out of society on religious grounds or even because of a belief in the importance of free enterprise and a mistrust for government. A full withdrawal would involve paying for private education, for a health plan, for toll roads everywhere, for a separate sanitation system; there would have to be a security network at all levels, too, including local policing and having a national and even an international dimension. A private army might even be necessary. We all receive a lot from the state, if we think about it. I'm reminded of that famous scene from Monty Python's film 'The Life of Brian' where the debt to Rome is spelled out: 'All right... all right... but apart from better sanitation and medicine and education and irrigation and public health and roads and a freshwater system and baths and public order... what have the Romans ever done for us?' Today, instead of each of us having to provide all of this individually, we pay taxes and that makes sense to me. Personally, I count it a privilege to pay tax and my only gripe is that I know some of the most wealthy in society don't feel the same. It seems to me that if everyone paid their fair share we'd all have the very best amenities.

The rest of the New Testament goes into some detail about the obligations the Christian has to society as a whole. The apostle Paul says that the powers that be are put in place by God and as such deserve our cooperation while elsewhere he says they ought to be able to count not only on our goodwill but our prayers. After all, he says, we get a quiet life and an opportunity to share the gospel when things are calm and smoothly run. This is not to say that we are to be indifferent to the nature of the government we have or remain silent when it is in our remit to call it to account, to influence it or to change it by taking part in elections. The Book of Revelation is amongst other things a stern critique of power and a clear word of condemnation against the use of force to persecute Christians. Personally, I would say that those who follow Christ should be attentive to the experience of of those who are suffering for their faith and be eager to call governments to account for their actions.

In short, we need to work hard to sort out the interface between rendering to Caesar and rendering to God. Jesus draws attention later in this chapter to a poor widow who, by contrast with the rich who give vast sums of money but who give nothing of their substance, gives everything she has. Each of us bears the image of God just as surely as every coin in our pockets bears the image of some figure of authority in our country. Everything we are and everything we have belongs to God who delegates plenty of functions to society to fulfil but others not, leaving them as he does to Christ's body here on earth to carry out. We are to worship God and make sure that the means to carry out corporate worship exist. We show compassion to those in need both around us at home and, as we become aware of them, in other lands. We witness to our faith where we live and make sure that we don't forget witness to those in other lands.

I want to finish this section with a story to illustrate how Caesar's coins may function in the Kingdom. In the seventeenth century in Bristol one of the leading Baptists was Edward Terrill who did well in trade in what was in this period the second city in England. These were turbulent times, though, and when Terrill came to be an elder of Broadmead Baptist Church in the 1660s, his congregation was persecuted. He negotiated and even fought long and hard with a church in London over a call issued by Broadmead to Thomas Hardcastle to come and be pastor in Bristol. Hardcastle had been educated in Cambridge University and had come to strong convictions as a vicar in the Church of England that did not allow him to stop preaching the gospel when he was removed from office in 1662. Until his death in 1678 and in spite of long periods of imprisonment Hardcastle continued faithful to his charge in Bristol. Terrill, for his part, was so impressed by what he had seen of an educated and zealous ministry that he was instrumental in founding Bristol Baptist College to train others for the task. To do this, he used his wealth made up of Caesar's coins and used the image of Caesar to honour the image of God.

Each of carries the image of Caesar on the currency in our pocket and we shouldn't be involved in trying to rob the society it represents of our contribution either in terms of our taxes or what we bring by way of gifts of personality and effort. By the same token, each of us carries the image of God in every part of our being and we shouldn't short-change him either.

Use your imagination (Luke 20:40-47)
The Old Testament is very extensively quoted in the New Testament in a wide variety of settings but, assuming they don't already know the answer to the question, most people would be hard-pressed to name the passage quoted the most frequently. It isn't Genesis on creation or on Abraham the father of faith, nor is it the sublime comfort of the twenty-third Psalm or even Isaiah's remarkable prophecies about the suffering servant of the Lord. In reality, and by a very long way indeed, the Old Testament extract with the most references is Psalm 110. Maybe that's quite a surprise: after all, there's not much beauty in it to make us desire it particularly and as we read it we are taken aback simply because we are nowhere near as sensitive to the issues it raises as people were in Bible times.

Psalm 110 is quoted by the apostle Peter on the day of Pentecost to explain God's vindication of the despised Jesus by his resurrection from the dead and it is used in the letter to the Hebrews to explain the pre-existence of Jesus as high priest even before his birth and his continuation in this role after rising from the dead. This Psalm is behind every New Testament assertion that Jesus is seated at the right hand of God and is even present in passages about the throne of God in Revelation.

Above all, though, Psalm 110 is the ground for debate chosen by Jesus himself during his last week of ministry and if he speaks at his trial of the Son of Man seated at God's right hand, then he is just continuing that teaching. So far, in that first Holy Week, we have observed Jesus the Outsider fielding questions and challenges from a variety of opposing parties in Judaism and he answers them in memorable ways, talking about Israel as God's vineyard, about the living faith of Abraham, Isaac and Jacob even though they have died and about Caesar's coin. When no one dares ask him any more questions, though, Jesus has one of his own which is an echo of the earlier query he put to his disciples: 'Who do people say I am, and who do you say I am?' It's a question he asks based on Psalm 110: 'Why is it said that the Messiah is the son of David . . . David calls him "Lord." How then can he be his son?'

The idea that the coming Christ would be in the lineage of David was quite a commonplace one at that time. The expectation of a king in David's line was everyone's hope and the basis for this hope realised in Jesus is something Luke goes out of his way to establish in the genealogy of Jesus given in chapter three. It's a theme Luke refers to repeatedly from the birth of Jesus in Bethlehem the city of David through the acclamation of Jesus as David's son by blind Bartimaeus shortly before the Palm Procession in Jerusalem. There, the expectant cries of the crowd resound with the same refrain. Later in the New Testament, Paul starts right there in Romans chapter one when he tells us that as far as his earthly life was concerned, Jesus was the son of David before being appointed the Son of God with power by his resurrection. There are preconceptions and mistaken hopes and longings for earthly influence built into the fact that Jesus was of the royal family of Israel but really all this is the ABC of what we call Christology.

In the first Holy Week, here was Jesus standing before the crowd as a man, with nothing particularly striking about his appearance and he turns to Psalm 110 - a talking-point of a psalm which was understood as being in some sense central to any understanding of the coming of the Christ. Jesus points to a very mysterious feature of this text when he mentions that David wrote it and in it observes a conversation between the Lord God and David's Lord. It is a conversation that portrays partnership and implies equality between these two figures of authority.

David's Lord was understood by all those listening to Jesus as being none other than the Christ and David does homage to him, drawing attention to a divine as well as to a human aspect to this mysterious figure. In the psalm, God elevates David's Lord to a place of honour which we are to understand not in a sense of subordination but in terms of equal honour. With the benefit of hindsight and perhaps with passages like the second chapter of Paul's letter to the Philippians in mind we think of Jesus living among us as one who serves and who after the cross is given a consort place alongside God.

We need to make a huge effort of the imagination now and try to put ourselves in the setting in Jerusalem in which this teaching of Jesus took place. Probably we come here with incomprehension because Psalm 110 doesn't excite and inflame us as it did the crowd. We also need to realise that Jesus had no special aura as a man except on one or two occasions when this broke through as at the Transfiguration and at the moment of his arrest in John's gospel. He was able to melt back into a hostile crowd; when they came to take him into custody he had to be identified with the secret signal of a kiss. We have a portrayal throughout the gospels of someone who could be tired, hungry and thirsty and who had dusty and sore feet himself when he knelt to refresh those of his proud disciples. Luke tells us that Jesus the Outsider unfavourably draws attention to the teachers of the law with their flowing robes, their long prayers and their outward honour but we have to confess that we are all too easily influenced by such considerations. When asked which group is more likely to represent God, a footsore, ragtag band of northerners from the sticks or the establishment figures of the Temple, we have to admit that we might jump the wrong way. The person standing before us making these grandiose claims looks just like you or me.

It takes faith to see in the Outsider Jesus the Lord to whom David gives homage and the high priest in the order of Melchizedek with neither beginning nor end of days. Faith like that can only come through the gift of the Holy Spirit and it is only available this side of the cross and resurrection. As it was, the claim of Jesus based on Psalm 110 only made the hostility of the Jerusalem authorities more acute.

A yellow Rolls-Royce (Luke 21)
It was in 1965 that I went with my family to London for the first time and everything was marvellous - of course it was: I was only six years old. I can still remember my first sight of Piccadilly Circus with its garish neon signs and even the spectacle of the Liverpudlian comedian Ken Dodd driving onto the stage of the London Palladium in a yellow open-top Rolls-Royce to begin his act is with me to this day. There was a funny incident when we were all crossing the busy road near Hyde Park Corner and my mother dropped a paper bag containing some 45 rpm records; the traffic thundered over them again and again

until the lights turned red and they could be retrieved. Miraculously, they were all intact except for one - 'Silence is golden' by Brian Poole and the Tremeloes. The crowning glory was Trafalgar Square with its lions and Nelson's Column. I did a drawing of that and sent it in to a well-known British children's television programme and proudly received a Blue Peter badge in return. Today, this trophy has pride of place fixed to my printer, although the clip on the back is long gone. London - there's no place on earth to compare with it.

The disciples felt the same way about their own capital, Jerusalem - we know that because this passage begins with them looking around the city with amazement. Who can blame them? They are outsiders - visitors from the provinces - and this was the beating heart of Judaism, the scene of so many great events and the place where God was held to have made his home. There are three very important and quite explicit lessons in this passage and, to state the obvious, the first is at the start, the second is in the middle and the third is at the end. They are separated by quite a lot of material that is not so important, though, so we need to tease these lessons out, identify them and underline them.

The first lesson is that nothing we can see is permanent - everything is passing. This applies not only to the Temple but to everything else as well and even though it is common sense, it is hard for us to grasp and needs to be spelled out. Shakespeare drew attention to this reality in The Tempest where in the context he is talking about his actors and the characters they represent in the play. His words apply to everything we can see, though:

'Our revels all are ended. These our actors as I foretold you were all spirits and are melted into air, into thin air
And like the baseless fabric of this vision the cloud capped towers the gorgeous palaces the solemn temples
The great globe itself yea all which it inherit shall dissolve and like this insubstantial pageant faded leave
Not a wrack behind. We are such stuff as dreams are made on and our little life is rounded with a sleep.'

The London of Shakespeare's day is gone. The London of our own day will disappear, too, as will any sight we hold dear in this world and even our very selves: in two hundred years time, Shakespeare's Prospero will live on in people's imagination when we are long forgotten. In terms of Jerusalem, some of the disciples will have lived long enough to see the fulfilment of Jesus's words about the destruction of the Temple in 70 AD by the Romans.

So, we need to live in the light of eternity and not invest ourselves too much in what we can see for the simple reason that treasure in heaven is worth far more than anything at all on earth. The division of the Bible into chapters and verses is only hundreds of years old, not thousands and the way it was done is not infallible but it was a stroke of genius to start this chapter with the poor widow making her tiny offering to the temple treasury. She is an apt illustration of someone taking eternity into account when life itself is precarious indeed.

The second lesson of this passage is in the middle of a lot of material that is not as important as some people think, people who feel that there is vital, factual information here about the end of the world. Just a few internet searches on this chapter will lead you to many hours of speculative reading about specific dates where you will learn amongst other things that the new planet discovered recently at the outer limits of our solar system was to have caused the destruction of earth in 2016 but that the authorities kept the news to themselves. You'll come away from your research more knowledgeable but none the wiser, as Fitzgerald put it in his translation of Omar Khayyam: 'Myself when young did eagerly frequent doctor and saint and heard great argument about it and about but evermore went out at the same door as in I went.'

My own belief about this vein of teaching of Jesus is that the revolutions and disasters he foretells are not specific ones but are constantly recurring and are meant to keep all Christians of all ages vigilant. The lesson is embedded in the teaching and is about reliance on the Holy Spirit: Jesus tells us that the Spirit will help us as we bear witness to our Christian faith because the Spirit is longing always and only for that testimony to go forward. This is not an invitation to think that if we are Christians somehow we have become infallible or that we have a special thing going with the Spirit that other Christians don't have. It is not an invitation to be foolhardy and to court danger for no real reason and certainly not an invitation to be boorish and opinionated. It is an invitation, though, to be open about faith in Jesus in the certain knowledge that the Spirit will support us and help us to speak.

The third lesson is about what our general outlook should be in view of the temporary nature of the world in which we live and in view of the impenetrable uncertainty of the date of the return of Jesus. About this teaching, there is no ambiguity at all: Jesus says: 'Be careful, or your hearts will be weighed down with carousing, drunkenness and the anxieties of life, and that day will close on you suddenly like a trap. For it will come on all those who live on the face of the whole earth. Be always on the watch, and pray that you may be able to escape all that is about to happen, and that you may be able to stand before the Son of Man.'

Jesus is telling us to be vigilant and not to be caught up too much in what we can see, be it Jerusalem or London. We are going to have to give an account of how our lives have been so it may as well be a good one. For each of us, though, how it looks will be quite unique to ourselves.

The fragrant cross (Luke 19:28 -23:56)

The last week of the ministry of Jesus before his death and resurrection is full of activity, noise and conflict and it begins on Palm Sunday when he rode into Jerusalem on a donkey to fulfil the prophecy of Zechariah: 'Behold, your king comes to you, humble and riding on a donkey.' The Bible reference of this acted parable wasn't lost on the crowd, who acclaimed him with songs and shouting, with palms and garments. What they didn't understand was that the rule of Jesus would not be marked by holy conquest and cleansing violence but by peace and self-sacrifice.

Next, Jesus went to the mighty Temple, maybe to witness its decay and mark it as fit for a destruction symbolised by the zealous overturning of the merchants' tables beneath the righteous wielding of a whip of cords.

Then comes a series of confrontations with all the parties in Judaism either one at a time or in combination and, above all in Matthew's gospel, the language used by Jesus is the strongest and most condemnatory in the New Testament. So much for, 'gentle Jesus, meek and mild' - he blazes with anger here. But the Pharisees, in particular, were so near to God and yet so far from him that they needed to be challenged - even the best religion when it goes bad is very dangerous indeed both for professor and those who are taught and it is at its worst when it blinds people to their need for God's mercy.

Events accelerate as the plot to do away with Jesus comes together and an informer is found and paid in advance of the sleepless, anguished night in the garden of Gethsemane where Jesus waits for the proverbial knock on the door at four in the morning. The kangaroo court is hastily convened and the disciples flee in fear for their lives - all their grandiose claims of loyalty had just been the big talk of little men boasting in their own strength.

The Friday after the Grand Sunday Arrival, Jesus is on the cross and it's all over by mid-afternoon but, even then, there is thunderous activity in the elements and the veil of the temple is torn in two. So, the last week of Jesus's ministry before his death and resurrection is full of activity, noise and conflict. All the same, we mustn't miss the moments of calm during this week, even though they, too, are shot through with agitation.

At the piano, I'm working on Beethoven's Pathetique Sonata with a vague idea of putting on a recital someday. This is a three-part work and the outer movements are all agitation but the slow movement in between is the heart of the work and it is blissfully quiet - even though there is the odd moment of anxiety even there. In this final, agitated week of Jesus's ministry before the cross and resurrection there are three places of calm - but each of them has pangs of anguish attached.

The first moment of calm is at the home of Mary, Martha and Lazarus at Bethany - here and at the Mount of Olives were the places where Jesus found peace and it's a great thing to have a base with good friends who are prepared to give us hospitality as to a family member. True, Jesus had raised Lazarus from the dead but it wasn't only gratitude that sparked this hospitality but love. It was in this house that Jesus was anointed by Mary with expensive perfume. What a beautiful action it was! But the pang was there because Judas couldn't bear to see the waste - in his gospel, John tells us he was motivated by money. This was a moment of calm for Jesus but the pang was the attitude of Judas.

In my last church, I did something that everyone there will remember for the rest of their lives when I brought a pint of perfume and poured it over the head of a willing volunteer. We can all testify that that fragrance remained on that person for months afterwards. We learned something that probably has never occurred to most people: at the cross Jesus was intensely fragrant with the perfume of Mary. As far as I can tell, this is my only original contribution to theology. As for the resurrection body of Jesus, I think it's idle to speculate on whether or not the fragrance lingered.

The second moment of calm is in the upper room at the Passover meal. In Judaism, the Passover is a family time when leisurely reflection on God's gracious actions in the Exodus from Egypt is done. For Jesus, the disciples are his family and he eagerly desires to eat this meal and think about God with them as he goes to his own exodus from the world.

In this upper room at that special meal, we see two actions that are at the centre of our Christian faith. First, in John's gospel, we see Jesus washing the feet of his disciples and telling them and us that we are to follow this example of humble service towards one another. The other action is in the other three gospels but not in John, as if John wanted to give us another slant on the events of that evening, perhaps assuming that we already know about Jesus leaving us the communion meal as our most important means of thinking about God's actions towards us. Just as the Jewish family gathers and, at Passover, goes through the events of the Exodus and reflects on belonging to God in the here and now, today we do the same thing but in a greatly simplified way in order to think about Jesus the fulfilment of the Jewish Passover.

I say that the communion meal is a simplified Passover observance because in Judaism there are four cups of wine with a reflection attached to each one: there are particular items placed on the table, too. There's a remnant of that more complex meal in Luke's account of the Lord's Supper which tells us about two cups of wine but from Matthew, Mark and Luke as a whole we retain just two elements: the bread broken to remind us of the broken body of Jesus and the one cup to remind us of his shed blood. These are two simple actions but they contain a world of reflection enough to nourish all of us throughout our Christian pilgrimage. The pang, once again, is provided by Judas. He was at the meal and we know that Jesus was aware of his heart of betrayal. In fact, Jesus knew that practically all of his disciples would run away in spite of their loud protestations of constancy, leaving only John and the women present at the foot of the cross.

I said there were three places of calm during this frenetic week of activity. The third is more abstract than the anointing by Mary and the communion meal: it is Jesus's knowledge that he is in the centre of God's will. Yes, the cross is ahead - this is the pang in this case - but the letter to the Hebrews tells us that 'for the joy that was set before him he endured the cross, despising the shame.' He was able to 'endure such contradiction from wicked men' because in the garden of Gethsemane, through tears and sweat, he won through to the place where he could say, 'nevertheless, not my will but yours be done.' Even in the depths of his ordeal, Jesus the Outsider know he was coming home.

There may be pangs of many kinds in our own lives, as Jesus

himself found, but there is a place of calm to be sought for us, too, in the centre of God's will.

This is about you (Luke 23 and 24)

I love Luke's gospel because this writer is concerned more than the others with outsiders, as I am myself - and I hope that what I feel is inspired by God's own heart. Over nearly thirty years, I have spent my ministry with people on the margins - with foreign guest workers in the opulence of Versailles, with homeless people and penniless African students in the balmy south of France: even here in a fairly affluent part of south Wales, I have always looked for those without many advantages. I have been back to France regularly, taking supplies to the refugees in the Calais Jungle in support of the Powers family.

I started preaching on Luke from this viewpoint some years ago, thinking I could cover most of the material in a month or two but in the end it took about two years and I still feel I'd like to go back through the gospel again looking for things I missed first time around. That series of sermons has turned into this book in which we have met a parade of losers according to the standards of the world - lepers, children, old people, the disciples, the Romans, women, Samaritans - but we have seen that they were all people that Jesus loved and sought to include in God's community by making them whole.

As I approached the end of the gospel, I came to wonder if Luke would follow through on this emphasis and whether he would be as concerned with outsiders at the end of his account as he was at the beginning. At the outset, there was a pregnant, unmarried girl who speaks an Overture of Overturning; there were shepherds, those homeless people earning a scanty living looking after the flocks of another; there was a disappointed priest and a childless woman who rejoice to see the Kingdom of God going forward through them. I wondered who would be there at the conclusion.

The first thing to be said is that on the cross, Jesus himself became the ultimate outsider. First, a terrible injustice was done and he was passed back and forth between Roman and Jewish authorities and then back to the Romans again for execution. The Letter to the Hebrews tells us to set our eyes on Jesus as the 'author and finisher' of our faith, even if this may involve the same kind of injustice for us that Jesus suffered. Next, Jesus was crucified alone with his followers watching from a safe distance and one of his closest friends suddenly rich from the windfall of betrayal, until that money began to weigh too heavily on his heart to be borne. Finally, in the biggest mystery of exclusion of all, we see the sun stop shining and the veil of the temple torn in two as Jesus cries out about being shut out from a lifetime of fellowship with his Father - 'My God, my God, why have you forsaken me?' Charles Wesley expressed all of our questions when he mused, 'Tis mystery all, the immortal dies! Who can explore his strange design? In vain the first-born seraph tries to sound the depths of love divine.'

And yet, the including grace of Jesus continues to operate even, in fact especially, from the cross. After all, a guilty man goes free as the terrorist and murderer Barabbas becomes the first to ask, 'Why should I gain from his reward . . . his wounds have paid my ransom.' A dying criminal at Jesus's side says, 'He has done nothing wrong' and thus becomes the first repentant sinner to enter paradise under the New Covenant even though he has no time to display fruits worthy of repentance. A Roman centurion, no less, is the first Christian preacher as he declares, 'Surely this was a righteous man.'

Gracious inclusion continues on Easter Sunday. The Jewish council members do not undergo a miraculous conversion after meeting with Jesus, although we learn from the rest of the New Testament that some came through to faith eventually. The Roman Empire does not suddenly become an instrument for spreading Christianity throughout the world - at least, not yet, not until the fourth century under Constantine. The disciples do not suddenly find hidden reserves of courage and emerge from hiding to rally to their executed leader. No, just as the centurion was the first preacher about the dying Christ by the cross, the women, denied a voice by the culture of the time, are the first evangelists as they bring the message of the risen Christ to the followers of Jesus in hiding who only then, in their turn, become witnesses. There are no big people in Luke's gospel, just little people who meet Jesus and come into the community of faith transformed. Mary's Overture of Inclusion becomes at the end a recapitulation of the themes announced there.

In the last chapter of Luke there is the little vignette of the walk to Emmaus. Once again, Luke has searched out this incident for us which the other writers know nothing about. We know the name of only one of the two disciples who are going there and who meet with a stranger who explains the scripture to them before being revealed in the breaking of the bread as Jesus himself. Cleopas is known to us and has his fifteen minutes of fame but the other disciple is so discreet as to be nameless, neither man nor woman, leaving no mark on history at all. Yet, you know that other disciple, for it is you yourself.

Like the unknown disciple on the road to Emmaus, you meet Jesus as you are simply going about your daily activities. You meet him as the Bible is opened and explained and you meet him in the breaking of bread in the life of the Church. Once, you were an outsider, too, but now you are included in the community of faith, even though you never knew Jesus according to the flesh.

How like Jesus that his last recorded words in this gospel bring together and extend the theme of excluded people in this gospel. They are spoken to the disciples together after the two from Emmaus had run back to Jerusalem after a weary day trudging in the opposite direction. These words are about those outside the camp in the whole world and about the power of the Holy Spirit on which we can count as we imitate Jesus and seek to reach out to those not yet included in his family. He says, 'This is what is written: The Christ will suffer and rise from the dead on the third day and repentance and forgiveness of sins will be preached in his name to all nations.'

Conclusion

As I come to the end of 'Luke Stranger', I thought I'd attempt some kind of closing reflection. I thought maybe it would be useful for readers to learn just a little about my own experience with outsiders like those who appear in Luke. So, my story is this: over many years I have been concerned with outsiders in society and in the church.

When I ministered in Versailles in the late 1980s and early 1990s, many of the congregation were Portuguese 'guest workers' who took care of the innumerable day to day tasks involved in keeping an affluent and fastidious community clean and functioning. Incidentally, it was at Versailles that I first came into contact with someone with Aids. A remarkable story of God's grace ensued but that will be for another time.

Later, in Toulouse, between and 1995 and 2002, I became involved with the homeless for the simple reason that there was a ragged man sleeping on the steps of our church until late in the day and I had to make a decision between trying to force t him to leave or inviting him in. By sharing coffee with him I discovered a new world for me with each new story of hard times being quite unique. I met a gifted jazz musician who would buy a guitar every month with his unemployment money, lose it in some drunken incident and then earn his money by whistling in the street. There was an estate agent, a cartoonist, a man fluent in a number of languages and with an impressive knowledge of world literature and philosophy but who would rave in the street. A fine-looking young man and woman who deteriorated before my eyes into toothless, hunched figures of fear in the inner city, known generally as, 'The couple from hell.'

For several years in Toulouse, I was involved with others in giving breakfast three times a week to sometimes as many as forty homeless people at one time in very cramped surroundings and with big dogs around. Towards the end of the morning, I would read the Bible and discuss it with a group of the people who came. There was no coercion to attend but those who did were happy for these sessions to go on for hours. I made a selection of readings from the New Testament as a monthly cycle for these discussions. At that time, I was endlessly frustrated because I wondered how long it would take for these people to join the church. By this, I meant start coming to Sunday services, perhaps be baptised and come into full membership of the fellowship. I wish I'd realised then that they were already in the church, maybe with a greater commitment than some of the more conventional attenders. It was a poor church - as the pastor, I was the only one with a car - and I used to joke that ours was the only fellowship I knew whose offering went down as the membership count went up - and that was even before the Sunday when one of the members stole the collection. It was only later that I came to realise that church is more than Sunday morning at eleven and that even though the accounts didn't look good, the experience had been very rich indeed.

It took my return to the UK in 2002 for me to come to understand that everything Christians do is Church - and that that includes leisure activities and what is done in the workplace as well as reading the Bible with the homeless. I came to this realisation by an unusual route, although I should also give due credit to the books of the Australian James Thwaites who wrote 'The Church beyond the Congregation' and 'Renegotiating the Church Contract'. So, I came to understand this in a surprising way: Sunday morning activities outside the church for children have become more and more of a drain on Christian families during my lifetime and the pressure to be involved in them is very hard indeed to resist for parents in church communities. I observed one family where the parents were vehement that their children would never skip church for football but who changed their minds in pretty short order when the boys were seen to have talent on the soccer field. I began a simple service for them before they left for the game, but I also began to affirm Christian presence at the match as Church activity. I refused to play the guilt card. Everything seemed to follow from that course of action.

I remember once in Toulouse giving a sermon series on Luke's gospel, focusing on the way Jesus brought back into the Judaism of his day people who were excluded from the system for one reason or another - perhaps because of lifestyle issues or an illness which rendered them ritually unclean. I think this is still a valid approach to Luke but nowadays I think the gospel writer's concern and that of Jesus himself is yet wider and speaks of God's love for all outsiders whether with regard to Judaism or more generally. Over the last two years of my ministry in Wales, I preached the substance of this 'Luke, Stranger' book and this reflection has helped me to see God active increasingly in all kinds of places.

While I have been back in Wales and under the influence of Thwaites and my own growing conviction that 'everything is church', my own activities have become more and more varied and less and less characteristic of what a Baptist minister traditionally does. My work as a piano and French teacher has been taking more and more of my time and I play in bands and have even taught a little theology in the university as well as sometimes giving 'thought for the day' type talks on BBC radio. I should point out that my church called me with the brief to be involved in the community and I have certainly done that. I am very grateful to the church for affirming me in what I have been doing. I also want to say that to be a piano teacher is a privileged role that brings you close not only to children but also to families: it has been a common occurrence for my expertise as a pastor to be called upon at some distance from the church community in some crisis of bereavement, illness, professional insecurity and so on.

The American preacher and writer A.W. Tozer used to say that because of his uncompromising teaching ministry he had preached himself off every platform in the United States. I think that, as I preached once again through Luke, this time focusing on the outsiders who throng its pages, I preached myself 'outside the camp' - in the words of the writer of the Letter to the Hebrews. I came to realise that my place now is not be inside the church looking out but on the borders of the church with no titles or position to disguise or obscure the fact that I am just an ordinary person who happens to be a Christian. That has been a liberation in itself and it feels like a good place.

I am still a Baptist minister, at least on paper, but I haven't preached or led a service except in France for a little while now. I am a man of far fewer words than I have ever been for thirty years and have been exploring a link with the Quakers that has been increasingly important to me for perhaps the last six or seven years. As well as a healthy respect for silence, the Quakers are activists in the quest for world peace and social justice, and I love that emphasis.

    I began to attend the Meeting for Worship of the Society of Friends on my free Sundays because I felt I needed an emphasis on silence and listening as a contrast to the welter of words and ideas with which a minister in the pulpit is involved. I must say, that the last full Baptist service I attended (I wasn't leading it) mystified me. I wondered what all these repetitive and, I felt, simplistic songs were for and why the prayers were so strangely disconnected with the world of refugees and Brexit and Trump which to me is central to any consideration of following Christ today. I wondered whether the person who preached with such animation really had that much to say about the Bible passage chosen. This is not meant to be dismissive or critical, by the way, and I am perfectly happy to ask the same questions of my own practice.

    Opportunities for ministry have not been lacking since stepping down from the church here so my long and expensive training and my decades of experience have not gone to waste as I initially feared they might. I continued to visit some members whom I have been helping for many years. What I said about getting alongside the piano pupils and their families when trouble comes continues to be true, unfortunately. The daily discipline of writing this book has clarified many things for me and when it was being published as a blog I valued the feedback I received as well as the thrill of sharing my thoughts on Luke with people in over thirty countries. I even ministered briefly in the Quaker meeting once, speaking with rare restraint for a Baptist minister for just one minute about the distinctive, silent contribution of the Friends to a national outpouring of prayer connected with the brutal murder of the British Member of Parliament, Jo Cox.

Perhaps most important of all were my trips to take supplies to the refugees in the Calais Jungle. Not everyone in my community agreed with this type of support and it sometimes felt an uncomfortable course of action in the painfully polarised debate over Brexit with its focus on immigration, but there is a good group of very compassionate people here who are happy to encourage these visits with gifts of clothes, food and even money.

On one trip, Charles Powers, my American friend who, as a minister in France, has found himself plunged into the midst of this humanitarian crisis, asked me to share with a group of young Iranians in their tent something of my own Christian journey. I think my colleague wanted me to speak about a conversion experience and I suppose I did in a way, because I found myself reflecting on the way God leads us sometimes imperceptibly in the long term rather than by any miraculous signs or spectacular specific guidance. As I shared earlier in the book, I told them about how my studies in French at university and my piano lessons as a boy with the elderly lady up the road (about whom I think every day as I teach) as well as theological study and thirty years of church ministry in the UK and then in France and finally back in Wales had brought me to that particular group of refugees in all of their fear and insecurity. I heard myself encouraging them with the thought that life is long and that the Calais Jungle is just one place and one time in their earthly pilgrimage. Other times and other places will become possible for them, whether in Teheran, London or New York.

Maybe, I was really speaking to myself - people tend to do a lot of that and I am no exception. These last few years have sometimes felt precarious but also strangely exhilarating: it takes a lot of faith to 'go into the church' but it takes a lot of faith to leave it, too. This conclusion of 'Luke, Stranger' is very much an interim report. That familiar verse from Exodus comes to my mind: 'You have made the sovereign Lord your refuge and underneath are the everlasting arms.' These words remind me that there is no escape from the love of God. All kinds of exclusion are practised by human beings and many of these are done in the name of religion, some in the name of Christ. With God himself, though, there is no excluding. 'The Son of Man came to seek and to save that which was lost' and there are many ways of coming home.

Printed in Poland
by Amazon Fulfillment
Poland Sp. z o.o., Wrocław